BAFFIN ISLAND
FRANKLIN
Home Bay
Davis Strait
GREENLAND (Den.)
PENNY HIGHLAND
Pangnirtung
CUMBERLAND PEN.
Cumberland Sound
C. MERCY
Nettilling
PRINCE CHARLES ISLAND
MELVILLE PENINSULA
Foxe Basin
Arctic Circle
Igloolik
Amadjuak
Frobisher Bay
HALL PEN.
Lake Harbour
EVERETT MTS.
RESOLUTION
FOXE PEN.
Foxe Channel
SALISBURY
Roes Welcome Sound
SOUTHAMPTON ISLAND
BELL PEN.
NOTTINGHAM ISLAND
Hudson Strait
C. WEGGS
C. HOPES ADVANCE
AKPATOK
CAPE CHIDLEY
TORNGAT MTS.
Nachvak
Hebron
Ungava Bay
Ivugivik
CAPE SMITH RANGE
UNGAVA PENINSULA
Payne
Ft. Chimo
Koksoak
Leaf
Fisher Strait
C. LOW
COATS
MANSEL
KEEWATIN
HUDSON BAY
All islands within bays and straits lie within Northwest Territories.
OTTAWA ISLANDS
Povungnituk
Minto
Kaniapiskau
Lac Bienville
BELCHER ISLANDS
Great Whale
Kaniapiskau
Schefferville
Nichicun
OTISH MTS.
Ft. Severn
C. HENRIETTA MARIA
Severn
Winisk
C. JONES
Fort George
James Bay
Ft. George
AKIMISKI
Opinaca
Eastmain
Rupert
Mistassini
Ft. Albany
Attawapiskat
Albany
Moosonee
Nottaway
Chibougamau
Moose
Martin Falls
Missinaibi
St. Joseph
Coral Rapids
Fraserdale
Mattagami
ONTARIO
QUEBEC
Lac Seul
Armstrong Sta.
Nakina
Hearst
Kapuskasing
Cochrane
Iroquois Falls
Timmins
La Sarre
Taschereau
Amos
Senneterre
Rouyn
Val-d'Or
Malartic
Kirkland Lake
Abitibi
Gouin Reservoir
Parent
La Tuque
Geraldton
Longlac
Oba
Nipigon
Dryden
Heron Bay
Franz
Chapleau
Timiskaming
Cobalt
Angliers
Ville-Marie
Timiskaming Sta.
MONTAGNE TREMBLANT PARK
QUETICO PARK
Fort William
Port Arthur
MICHIPICOTEN I.
Lake Superior
Sault Ste. Marie
Thessalon
Blind River
Espanola
Sudbury
Sturgeon Falls
Mattawa
North Bay
Nipissing
ALGONQUIN PARK
Pembroke
Renfrew
Ottawa
Huntsville
Bancroft
Smiths Falls
Parry Sound
Georgian Bay
GEORGIAN IS. NAT'L PARK
MANITOULIN
Lake Huron
Orillia
Peterborough
Midland
Barrie
Lindsay
Oshawa
Whitby
Cobourg
Trenton
Kingston
Brockville
Toronto
Lake Ontario
Hamilton
Niagara Falls
Buffalo
Rochester
Wiarton
Owen Sound
Kincardine
Wingham
Goderich
Woodstock
Brantford
London
Simcoe
St. Thomas
Sarnia
Port Huron
Chatham
Windsor
Leamington
Lake Erie
DETROIT
Flint
Lansing
Saginaw
Grand Rapids
Milwaukee
Madison
Lake Michigan
Green Bay
Escanaba
Marquette
Sault Ste. Marie
Superior
St. Paul
Mississippi
Wisconsin
UNITED STATES
MONTREAL
Lachine
Lacolle
Valleyfield
Joliette
Sorel
St. Hyacinthe
Granby
St. Jean
Magog
Sherbrooke
Shawinigan
Grand Mère
Trois Rivières
Victoriaville
Asbestos
Lac Mégantic
Quebec
Lévis
St. Maurice
Chicoutimi
Jonquière
Saguenay
Dolbeau
Roberval
St. Félicien
Alma
Kenogami
Chambord
LAURENTIDES PARK
La Malbaie
Baie St. Paul
Péribonca
Mistassibi
Betsiamites
R. aux Outardes
Manicouagan
St. Lawrence River
Clarke City
Sept-Îles
Moisie
Mingan
ANTICOSTI
Ashuanipi
Labrador City
Attikonak
Little Mecatina
Natashquan
Romaine
Harrington Harbour
LABRADOR
NEWFOUNDLAND
HOPE MTS.
MEALY MTS.
Michikamau
Naskaupi
Goose Bay
Grand Falls
Melville
Rigolet
Hamilton Inlet
Cartwright
Battle Harbour
Makkovik
Hopedale
Nain
ATLANTIC OCEAN
Strait of Belle Isle
St. Anthony
LONG RANGE MTS.
Corner Brook
Stephenville
St. George
Port-aux-Basques
Gulf of St. Lawrence
MAGDALEN ISLANDS
CAPE BRETON HIGHLANDS NAT'L PARK
Glace Bay
Sydney
Sydney Mines
New Waterford
Louisburg
Hawkesbury
Canso
Cap-Chat
NOTRE DAME MTS.
Gaspé
GASPÉ PEN.
Matane
Mont-Joli
Rimouski
Chandler
New Carlisle
Chaleur Bay
Caraquet
Campbellton
Bathurst
Rivière du Loup
Edmundston
Newcastle
Chatham
Richibucto
St. John
NEW BRUNSWICK
P.E.I.
PRINCE EDWARD NAT'L PARK
Charlottetown
Summerside
New Glasgow
Amherst
Stellarton
Springhill
Truro
Moncton
Fredericton
Sussex
FUNDY NAT'L PARK
Saint John
St. Andrews
St. George
St. Stephen
Woodstock
Lac Frontière
NOVA SCOTIA
Windsor
Dartmouth
Halifax
Kentville
Lunenburg
Bridgewater
Liverpool
Digby
Bay of Fundy
Yarmouth
Shelburne
CAPE SABLE
Augusta
Portland
Montpelier
Champlain
Ogdensburg
ST. LAWRENCE IS. NAT'L PARK
Alexandria Bay
Concord
Boston
CAPE COD
Providence
Hartford
Albany
Connecticut
Hudson
LONG ISLAND
NEW YORK
Scranton
Jersey City
Trenton
PHILADELPHIA
Gulf of St. Lawrence
Strait of Belle Isle
St. Anthony
LONG RANGE MTS.
White Bay
C. ST. JOHN
Notre Dame Bay
Twillingate
Deer Lake
Humbermouth
Corner Brook
Stephenville
C. ST. GEORGE
Botwood
Windsor
Grand Falls
Gander
Bonavista Bay
Bonavista
TERRA NOVA NAT'L PARK
Grand
Red Indian
NEWFOUNDLAND
St. George's Bay
St. George's
Trinity
Trinity Bay
CAPE RAY
Cabot Strait
Port-aux-Basques
Bay Roberts
Wabana
St. John's
Placentia Bay
Fortune Bay
Grand Bank
Burin
CAPE NORTH
MIQUELON (Fr.)
ST. PIERRE (Fr.)
CAPE BRETON ISLAND
ATLANTIC OCEAN
©RMCN
80° 75° 70° 65° 60° 55° 50° 45° 40° 90° 85°

LIFE WORLD LIBRARY

CANADA

LIFE WORLD LIBRARY
LIFE NATURE LIBRARY
TIME READING PROGRAM
THE LIFE HISTORY OF THE UNITED STATES
LIFE SCIENCE LIBRARY
INTERNATIONAL BOOK SOCIETY
GREAT AGES OF MAN
TIME-LIFE LIBRARY OF ART
TIME-LIFE LIBRARY OF AMERICA
FOODS OF THE WORLD

LIFE WORLD LIBRARY

CANADA

by Brian Moore

and the Editors of

TIME-LIFE BOOKS

TIME-LIFE BOOKS NEW YORK

COVER: Wheat fields
in Saskatchewan dwarf the
men and machines which till them
as they stretch uninterrupted
toward a distant horizon.

ABOUT THE WRITER

Brian Moore, who wrote the interpretive chapters for this volume of the LIFE World Library, emigrated to Canada from his native Belfast, Ireland, in 1948 and lived there for 11 years before moving to the U.S. While in Canada he worked for the Montreal *Gazette* as a reporter and traveled widely writing articles on Canada for other publications. His principal works, however, are five novels: *The Feast of Lupercal, The Lonely Passion of Judith Hearne, The Luck of Ginger Coffey, An Answer from Limbo* and *The Emperor of Ice-Cream. The Luck of Ginger Coffey,* a tragicomic story about the trials of an Irish immigrant to Canada, received the Governor-General of Canada's Award for fiction in 1960. Mr. Moore has also received a Canada Council fellowship and a Guggenheim fellowship. He is now living in California.

Published simultaneously in Canada.
Library of Congress catalogue card number 63-21908.
School and library distribution by Silver Burdett Company.

Contents

The text for this book was written by Brian Moore and the picture essays by David S. Thomson. The following individuals and departments of Time Inc. gave valuable aid in the preparation of this book: LIFE staff photographers Alfred Eisenstaedt, Fritz Goro, Ralph Morse, Carl Mydans and George Silk; contributing photographer Richard Meek; the Chief of the LIFE Picture Library, Doris O'Neil; the Chief of the Bureau of Editorial Reference, Peter Draz; the Chief of the TIME-LIFE News Service, Richard M. Clurman; Correspondents Ed Ogle (Calgary), Serrell Hillman (Toronto), Marsh Clark (Ottawa) and Robert Lewis (Montreal); the Editor of TIME's Canadian Edition, John M. Scott; the former Managing Director of Time International of Canada, Ltd., Lawrence E. Laybourne.

Introduction

Mr. Brian Moore does a needed service in this book about Canada. He writes with sure knowledge and sympathetic understanding of our northern neighbor, and the pictures interlaced with the text capture the broad sweep of Canada, its beauty and its loneliness.

For most of us in the United States, Canada is not really a foreign country. And failure to grasp this simple fact accounts for much of the difficulty which growingly attends our relationship. If we are to understand Canada—as in our deepest self-interest we must—then we have to accept the fact that Canadians want to be Canadians and not "Americans." They want to cultivate their own distinctive national personality and culture—which is under the casual but constant bombardment of a nation 10 times more populous and 13 times richer.

The fact that this steady bombardment of the printed word, of movies, radio and television, of labor unions, of capital seeking investment and of ideas in general is wholly casual, and not the calculated penetration of Canada by the United States government for a political purpose, has really nothing to do with the case. The Canadians are where they are—next to us—and in order to resist the pressures to which they feel subjected, they will perpetually amaze most of us in the United States by their reactions to what we do or say to them in all innocence. Even more difficult for most of us to understand is the fact that they feel most injured when we do or say nothing to them—for then "we are taking Canada for granted."

It is because of this abyss of innocence—even ignorance—on our side of the border that Mr. Moore does such valiant service. He better enables a wide audience in our own country to understand something of the proud history and the uncertain, troubled vision of a distinctively Canadian destiny held by our friends in that rich, varied, empty, beautiful country that is Canada.

The penetration of the wilderness by the early voyageurs; the opening up of the rich prairies; the achievement first of Confederation in 1867 and then in 1931 of independence under the Crown; the legendary heroism of Canadians in two world wars and more recently in Korea; the industrialization that has come in recent decades; and the remarkable role that Canada began to play on the world stage after World War II, in the United Nations, in the Commonwealth, in NATO and indeed everywhere that a few nations gathered together—all these constitute a tribute to the character, the ability and the independent-mindedness that Canada breeds.

Different as Canadians are from us and as they are determined to remain, many readers of this volume (and this introduction) will no doubt continue to cling to the belief that their Canadian relatives and business associates and vacation companions could not possibly be so unfriendly as to fail to take pride in being mistaken for "Americans." If, however, even a few readers are led to re-examine this conviction, this book will have done its part to serve well the future relations of the two peoples who by geography, history, trade, science and modern communications have been made truly interdependent.

LIVINGSTON T. MERCHANT
former U.S. Ambassador to Canada

Before a backdrop of Montreal towers, the multilevel "Habitat" apartment complex, designed by Moshe Safdie, extends along an island

in the St. Lawrence. It was Expo 67's most distinctive structure.

1

The Land God Gave to Cain

THE transcontinental jet lifts into the morning skies over Vancouver airport and turns inland away from the Pacific Coast. The stewardess announces in American accents that the flight is en route to London, England, via Gander in Newfoundland. She then repeats her announcement in a strangely accented French. The passengers, too, seem a little odd. They look and dress like Americans, but there is a European touch in their orderly manners, in their durable overshoes and sensible woolly scarves. Obediently, they accept magazines and settle down to read. A few look out at the Rocky Mountains, now scattered below the plane like the teeth of a tyrannosaur in a bleak, prehistoric landscape.

The passengers are Canadian, members of the first generation of their country that is able, in a single day, to see something of the outline of this enormous land. Their parents, traveling coast to coast by train, were, by comparison, blind people feeling their way across the rump of a mammoth. Even today, most strangers are unaware of Canada's sheer physical size. How many Americans or Europeans realize that it is the second largest country in the world, exceeded in size only by the Soviet Union? Or that it has more lakes than the rest of the world combined? And that while it contains one of the world's last great undeveloped areas, it is, paradoxically, the sixth largest trading nation on earth? Someone once surmised that a thing might be so big as to be invisible. Canada would seem to prove the point. It is, indeed, invisible. No one, living or dead, has ever seen it whole.

It is also safe to suppose that our Canadian jet passengers, placidly engrossed in the latest issues of LIFE, *The Saturday Evening Post* or *Maclean's* (a Canadian periodical), are only vaguely aware of these statistics and care for them not at all. Canadians are not chauvinistic about their country's size and are sometimes apologetic about its past. Unlike the citizens of other countries, they look back on no history of revolution, wars of independence or great political crises. Only since 1965 have they saluted their own flag; for years they were unable to agree on a distinctive national ensign. Their real history has been a battle against an enemy symbolized by the implacable mountains they now fly over: if a small plane should crash among those peaks and valleys, it might be six months before it was discovered. Their enemy is climate and geography: their battle is not yet won.

FLOWN over at a height of 30,000 feet, the Canadian Rockies (wilder and more impassable than the American Rockies to the south of them) end as abruptly as the corrugated welts on a schoolroom globe and are replaced by a seemingly endless parquetry floor of blacks and dull browns. To passengers from British Columbia these prairies are strange territory, another country which they may not know and may possibly never visit. For if size is the first cardinal fact about Canada, regional isolation is the second. A quick glance at a topographical map of North America will show that the boundary between Canada and the United States is artificial, an arbitrary line. The natural divisions of the continent run north to south. Men, like birds, migrate south, and so it has been estimated that, for every two Canadians who have visited an adjoining eastern or western province in Canada, four have visited the region of the United States immediately to the south of their own.

OUR jet plane, having crossed the mountain wall which divides the rich lumber and farming areas of British Columbia from the wheatlands of the Prairie provinces, must, on leaving the Prairies, fly over a new barrier, a thousand-mile block of wilderness—rock, water and tree—before reaching the industrialized and heavily populated regions of Ontario. Ontario is separated from its neighboring province of Quebec not by a natural barrier but by the French language and by the memory of almost two centuries of mutual distrust. As our jet flies over southern Quebec, it will approach a crooked elbow of northern New England, gerrymandered long ago by the British to keep the troublesome French Canadians from commanding an outlet to the Atlantic Coast.

The plane will fly over the Atlantic Maritime region, and when it reaches the airport at Gander and sets down in Newfoundland, the 10th and most recent province to join confederated Canada, it will already have left the mainland, for Newfoundland proper is an island, long treated by its British rulers as "a great ship moored near the [Grand] banks during the fishing season, for the convenience of English fishermen." The plane will have flown 3,300 miles, passed through six time zones and traversed the great natural boundaries that separate the major regions of Canada. Walls, both physical and political, have always partitioned this enormous land, turning its citizens' gaze inward, fixing their minds on local loyalties, local faiths.

Some years ago a big Canadian distilling company, searching for ideas for a promotion

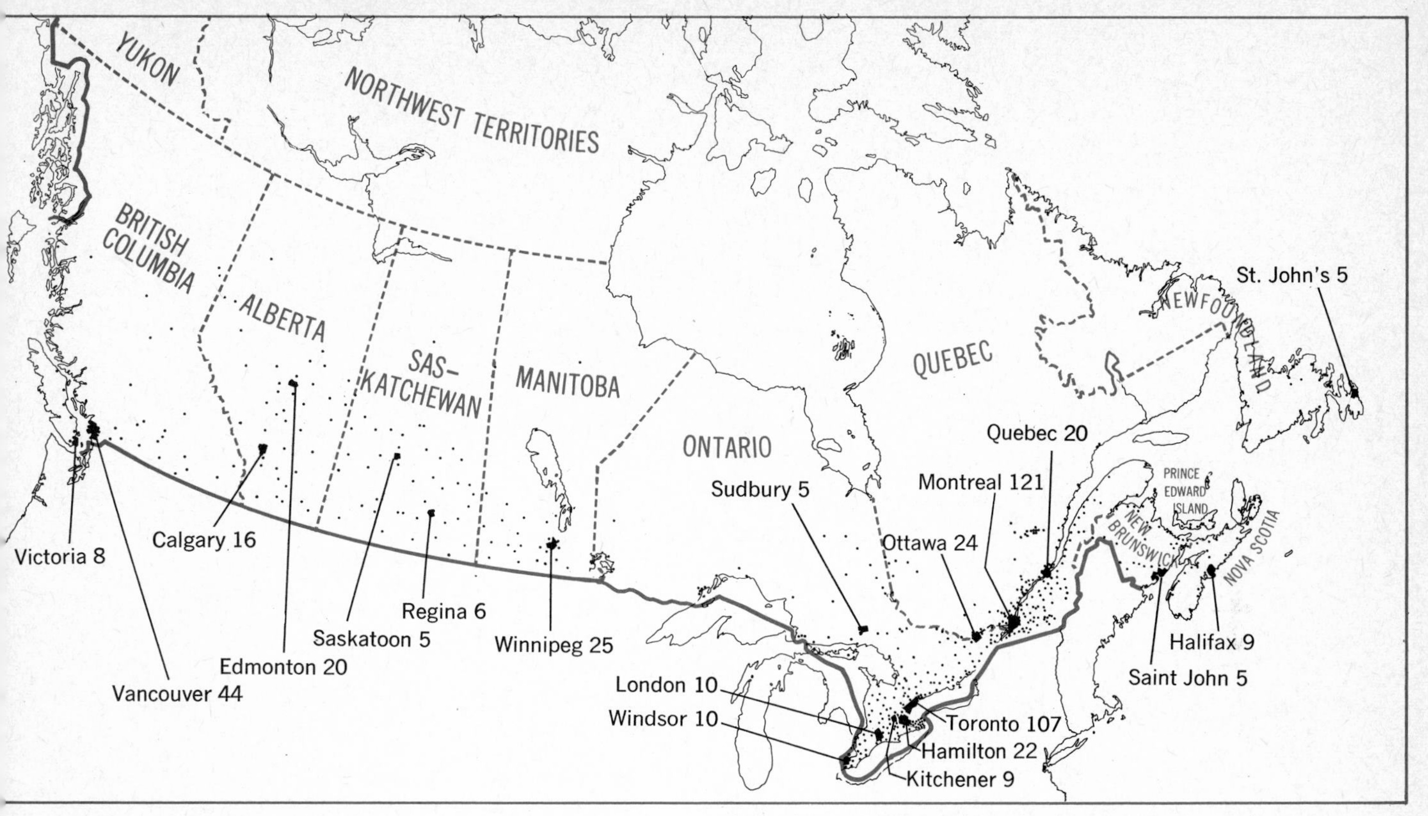

CANADA'S POPULATION is concentrated along the southern edge of the country, just above the U.S. border. In this map, each dot represents 20,015 people, or 1/1,000 of the nation's population in 1966. The numbers shown represent the total dots which would be present in certain urban areas, i.e., the Montreal area's 1966 population was 121 dots, or 2.4 million.

campaign that would not offend those provinces which frown on liquor advertising, decided that patriotism was the perfect theme. On buses and streetcars signs appeared bearing the slogan: THE ONLY ISM FOR CANADIANS IS CANADIANISM. The fact that the company's advertising trademark, a parrot, was shown beside the slogan raised no flicker of satirical comment in any Canadian newspaper or magazine. Canadians simply ignored the advice. For, unlike Americans, they have rarely been indoctrinated with official appeals for patriotism, nor has the country made any real effort to become a "melting pot" or a haven for Europe's poor and dispossessed. Five out of six Canadians today were born in Canada and the majority are still of British or French stock.

The French stock is the oldest, amounting to about 30 per cent of the total, and French Canadians have successfully resisted all efforts to merge their language and customs with the dominant Anglo-Saxon culture. One of the most striking differences between Canada and the United States is that in Canada one fifth of the population speaks French only. British and U.S. stock amounts to about 50 per cent of the total population. The remaining 20 per cent comes mainly from continental Europe. The great majority of this group learns English, rather than French. Their children go to English-speaking schools and eventually merge into the Anglo-Saxon culture. Canadians, if asked to define Canadianism, usually do so in negative terms. It is not Americanism, they say. And equally, they insist, they are not British or French.

Yet to the rest of the world, including England, France and the United States, Canadians *do* seem like Americans. Their cars, their food, their clothes, their plumbing are in the American manner. They play American-style football instead of Rugby, stay immobile beside their television sets during the World Series, read American columnists like Art Buchwald and Ann Landers, and become Shriners, Elks, Rotarians and Kiwanians. They speak with accents more American than British (even the French Canadian, when he learns English well, sounds more American than French). One of their peculiar conceits is that they have *no* accent, which really means that there is remarkably little variation in Canadian accents from coast to coast.

Canadians traveling abroad are, therefore, in the curious position of constantly being taken for Americans, and this often has a chastening effect on their own brand of anti-Americanism. When forced to explain themselves as Americans to a hostile audience, they frequently discover that they have much more in common with the people of the United States than they had imagined. It irritates them when English people say, "You Americans," in sneering tones and then, being informed that they are Canadians, promptly apologize: "Oh, I'm *so* sorry. I thought you were a Yank." Stung, the Canadian usually replies: "So what if I was? You'd think being American was a disease or something, to hear you people talk. Let me tell you...."

In fact, Canadians are North Americans, and the citizens of the United States are their closest cousins. Possibly the only definition of Canadianism that some citizens might agree on is the wry observation that "a Canadian is someone who has turned down a chance to go and live in the United States." Until fairly recently, there were no stringent laws to stop Canadians and Americans from moving freely across the international border and settling where they chose. Even today, no quota exists to hamper the admission of native-born Canadians to live and work in the United States. The price of remaining in Canada is the acceptance of a standard of living somewhat lower than the American and payment of an annual bill for Canadian consumers of around $500 million in tariffs imposed by the Canadian government on goods imported from the United States.

However, as this still leaves Canada with the third highest standard of living in the world (Sweden's is second), Canadians have, in the past, been condescending about those of their number who have defected to the richer pastures in the south. But in a new wave of self-criticism which is now sweeping the country, some tremors of self-doubt are discernible. Professor A.R.M. Lower, a leading Canadian historian, believes that "it has tended to be the more able, and especially the spontaneous, the extroverts, 'the up-and-coming,' who have gone to the United States. . . . Canada has retained the withdrawn people, the sedate, and those with the least energy and ability."

This image of Canadians as inert is not new. In 1776 Lord Carleton, the English governor of Lower Canada, said of them: "I think there is nothing to fear from them while we are in a state of prosperity and nothing to hope for while in distress." And Rupert Brooke, the English poet, who took an extensive tour of North America in 1913, wrote that "Canada is a live country, live, but not, like the States, kicking." Canadians, however, are little ruffled by such charges. To them, extrovert equals "show-off" equals American.

They have always been curiously allergic to heroes or men of remarkable accomplishments,

CANADA'S REIGNING MONARCH

Despite Canada's complete political autonomy, the Queen of England is still officially the country's ruler. The British North America Act of 1867 provides that "the Executive Government and authority of and over Canada is . . .vested in the Queen," and this provision still stands. The Queen's real power, however, is virtually nonexistent, being confined to such matters as instituting new military decorations or laying cornerstones. The Crown's Canadian representative, the governor-general (likewise powerless), who fulfills the important symbolic function of head of state, is now always a Canadian. During royal visits, the Queen performs duties usually dispatched by the governor-general in her name, such as opening or closing Parliament. Canadians of non-British descent are increasingly restive with this symbol of the country's colonial past.

and while their history is staked out with romantic rebels like Louis Riel (who led a tragic rebellion of French-Indian half-breeds against government mounted police in 1885 and became a symbol of French-English conflict), colorful figures like Prime Minister Sir John A. Macdonald (who unified the provinces of Canada under Confederation) and selfless scientists like Sir Frederick Banting (who handed over for scientific research all royalties due him for his discovery of insulin), Canadians have indulged in little hero-worship. The status of hero is generally reserved for sports figures, usually the top scorer in the National Hockey League. Not long ago a riot was touched off in Montreal by the suspension of the great forward of the Canadiens hockey team, Maurice (Rocket) Richard, from the Stanley Cup play-offs for bashing an official who sought to prevent him from bashing a Boston player. Enthusiastic fans have even elected a number of hockey players as Members of Parliament.

THE quintessential Canadian public figure was the late William Lyon Mackenzie King, a colorless bachelor who held the post of prime minister of his country for an astonishing total of 21 years. (His span of office covered roughly the years 1921-1948, with two short periods—three months in 1926 and five years in the early 1930s—when the rival Conservative party was in power.) Yet King appeared on the world stage only as one of the dim figures seated with British monarchs at Commonwealth conferences, or as a formal, sometimes unidentified, third in news photographs of Winston Churchill and Franklin Delano Roosevelt at the wartime Quebec Conference. In his shrewd manipulation of parties and parliaments, however, he was easily Roosevelt's equal as a politician, and in jockeying for advantage in Commonwealth affairs he coolly took the measure of Churchill's florid rhetoric.

King, in his public persona, seemed to embody all the traits which Canadians have approvingly owned up to. It has been said that Canada has a weak revolutionary, or radical, strain and a strong counter-revolutionary, or conservative, one. Canadians have further been described as having "a shrewd sense of the possible" and "an inescapable sense of limitations." They see themselves as defenders of responsible government and as naturally obedient to law and order. King seemed all these things and, in addition, personified the frontier virtues of canniness and toughness in a time of crisis. Yet when he died the public learned that this lonely man was a secret spiritualist, a believer in mediums, a gazer into crystal balls. In his combination of shrewd practicality and hidden uncertainty, he is perhaps the most startling example of that dichotomy which governs the Canadian character.

Something of this uncertainty is reflected in the Canadian attitude to cities. Canadians have never formed a strong attachment to one chief city, though they have a fierce regional civic pride. Because of this, Canada has no single metropolis to which the ambitious and talented inevitably migrate. The larger cities do not even interconnect in a cultural sense but remain, for the most part, distinct regional capitals mirroring their own surrounding area. Montreal, the largest city, offers the best food and entertainment; Toronto is the seat of the publishing and communications industries. But neither is in a satellite position to the other. As for the capital, Ottawa, its site on the border between Quebec and Ontario, the two most populous provinces, was chosen by Queen Victoria's ministers mainly to avoid offending either province. Ottawa remains a one-industry civil service factory, a small town whose business is government.

IN building their cities, Canadians, practical as always, chose sites which were useful to trade in or to fight from; happily, these sites are often in surroundings of great natural beauty. Vancouver is on a huge Pacific coastal strait, backed by snow-topped mountains. Toronto is pleasantly situated on the shores of Lake Ontario. Montreal is sited on the lower slopes of a fine hillside which overlooks the St. Lawrence River. Quebec, also on the St.

Lawrence, sits high on imposing cliffs, rather like a medieval citadel, and Halifax lies along the beautiful coastline of Nova Scotia, in one of the world's finest natural harbors.

Alas, the practical Canadians saw these cities as largely utilitarian and they remain so. There is something makeshift in their composition, and the Canadian dislike of show results in a drab absence of civic gaiety. And while Canadian homes on the inside are usually efficient machines for living, their outward appearance often suggests neglect. A visitor driving across the border from upstate New York or New England is at once struck by hideous vistas of unpainted walls and fences, ill-kempt lawns and a rash of unchecked advertising billboards. Canadian small towns, with their hodgepodge clutter of gimcrack stores, neon signs and overhead wiring, are sometimes unsightly enough to make Jersey City, New Jersey, look like a town-planner's paradise.

Canadians are likely to turn away such criticisms with the truthful statement that other countries do not have to cope with the harsh Canadian climate. In most cities and towns, ice cracks the pavements with seasonal regularity. In the East, snow-clearance bills can run into millions (Montreal has an average annual snowfall of about 100 inches). But the real indifference to outward appearances seems to stem from a frontier attitude, an ingrained sense of impermanence reinforced by the brutal truths of geography.

UNTIL 1962 there was no highway which stretched from coast to coast across the country, and Canadians going from east to west by car were obliged to dip down across the border and drive through stretches of the U.S. Even today, the new Trans-Canada Highway, a slender 5,000-mile ribbon of paved road linking St. John's, Newfoundland, with Victoria, British Columbia, is only two lanes wide over most of its length. In addition, the overwhelming majority of Canada's 20 million people live in a narrow belt of country, not more than 200 miles wide, which huddles along the border with the United States. At almost no point can a Canadian get in his car and drive 150 miles north without coming face to face with the real Canada—the wilderness.

The wilderness is some two and a half million square miles of dwindling forests, arctic tundra and the rock, ice and snow of the arctic archipelago. Its vegetation varies from huge and ancient conifers to the ground flowers of the tundra, which bloom almost with the speed of a Disney nature film in the brief arctic summers of almost nightless days. It is a land which is virtually uninhabited, a land in which Indian and Eskimo once led a nomadic existence as in a great desert, a land knit today only by the most attenuated thread of air, rail and water routes. Oil and mineral wealth has already been discovered in some areas, and in the minds of Canadian politicians the region remains "an unopened safety deposit box on the future."

MOST of this crude mineral wealth lies in the Canadian Shield, one of the oldest and most worn portions of the earth's crust, which spreads out across the country in a huge horseshoe from the great watery fist of Hudson Bay. It is a land where all but a few of the ancient mountains have been worn down to stumps, a land where soil is thin or nonexistent except in the vast, soggy lowlands. The wrinkles and hollows of this shield are filled with uncounted lakes, rivers and streams, huge deserts of muskeg swamp and soaking beaver meadows. The shield covers about one half of the total area of Canada and has changed little since 1534, when Jacques Cartier, the French explorer, sighting it at its eastern extremity in the Strait of Belle Isle between Newfoundland and Labrador, turned his ships southward from its awesome face, saying, in words echoed by Canadians ever since: "I believe that this was the land God gave to Cain."

Bleak it may be, but it is not barren. Within the shield are quantities of copper, iron, gold, silver, zinc, nickel, titanium, uranium, platinum and lithium. These materials—along with oil and natural gas found elsewhere—have changed Canada from an agricultural to an industrial nation and are responsible for much of the population growth.

But, to survive in this land, men must indeed have "a shrewd sense of the possible" and "an inescapable sense of limitations." A writer for the Canadian National Film Board tells of portaging supplies up the remote and terrifying Virginia Falls in the Northwest Territories in the company of a 72-year-old Canadian prospector. For almost a week the tenderfoot and the old-timer labored to carry their supplies to the top of the 316-foot falls where they would build a new and smaller boat to navigate the upper rapids. On the last day, on the last trip, two small boxes of supplies remained when both men were loaded for the final climb. "We'll come back down for it tomorrow," the old prospector said. The writer was irritated and offered to carry the extra boxes. The old man refused to let him do it. "The only way to stay alive in this country," he said, "is never to do anything above your strength."

But, coupled with this animal sense of limitations, Canadians have a refreshing absence of pompousness and a genuine frontier friendliness that makes them equally popular with both Americans and Britons. For they are neither so reserved as to seem cold, nor so ebullient as to appear tiresome. In a real way, the Canadian seems the North American Everyman, open and unaffected, at home with people wherever he meets them.

CANADIANS, with their quiet voices and pleasant social manners, were known as "The Quiet Americans" long before the British novelist Graham Greene used the title in a novel describing a very different sort of quietness. Their popularity in the United Nations, especially among the uncommitted countries, stems from a feeling that they are dependable and just. And if strangers sometimes wonder at their unwillingness to make flamboyant gestures or sacrifices, it must be remembered that inhabited Canada is like the basement of an enormous mansion, filled with untested stairways, unlit corridors, unknown rooms. The Canadians move cautiously, even in the basement. If their politics tend to be provincial rather than federal, if they seem to lack dash and a nationalistic fervor, it may be that this is a necessary condition for their survival.

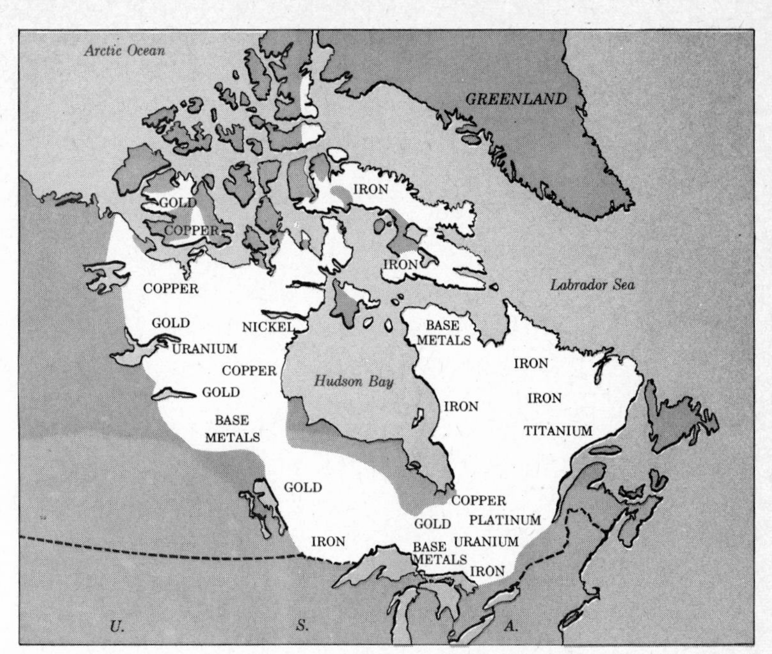

THE CANADIAN SHIELD, a huge area surrounding Hudson Bay, has been called "the mineral storehouse of the nation." Most currently active mines are located on the shield's edge.

Even their unwillingness to cheer any hero other than the false hero of sports—whose risks are calculated and limited—is, perhaps, a reflection of the harsh facts of geography and climate. There are no heroes in the wilderness. Only fools take risks.

But risks still exist, and this is being brought home, frighteningly, to the whole nation. For today, a century after Canada's Confederation, the country is so rent by old ethnic divisions, threatened in its independent economic survival and lit with alarms that its very existence as a nation is now in jeopardy. In these risks and fears there is reflected, perhaps, the uneasy tenancy of a country too big, too terrifying for man's mind to grasp and conquer. Canada is so big as to seem invisible. And man has always feared the unknown.

The Provinces' Vast Sweep from Coast to Coast

Canada is an immense and, for the most part, lonely land. But, considering the country's size and the relatively brief time it has been settled, its people have managed to make a remarkable impress on their wild domain. The story of this effort can be read in a trip through Canada from coast to coast, from the fishing villages of the Maritime provinces and the old, settled cities on the St. Lawrence River to the broad Prairie wheat fields and finally to the fast-developing areas of the West Coast. However, the wilderness remains—vast tracts of unexplored forest and Arctic tundra which resist man's civilizing hand and may do so forever.

NOVA SCOTIA FISHERMEN stand on a tidal flat near the port of Blue Rock to discuss the day's catch. Nova Scotia's fisheries remain important to the province's economy, employing some 12,600 men, although the days when Nova Scotia possessed one of the world's largest mercantile fleets are long since gone. The province was first settled by the French in 1604.

NEWFOUNDLAND FISHING SHACKS perch on the edge of Bonavista Bay *(opposite),* where fishermen's children play with a blanket near an abandoned stove. Virtually all of Newfoundland's villages were once coastal, and the tiny ports sent fleets of ships to the Grand Banks, but recently a drive has been made to settle the interior and to develop new industries.

THE SETTLED EAST, typified by Quebec and Montreal, has an air of permanence reminiscent of yesterday's Europe

A handsome park offers lunchtime repose in Montreal's

ANCIENT RAMPART of Quebec's Citadel provides a walk for visitors *(left)* as a sentry guards a garrison mess. In the background is the Château Frontenac Hotel.

WINDING STAIRWAY, making a handsome backdrop for a children's game, curves gracefully down the outside of an old balconied house *(above)* in the Verdun section of Montreal.

Dominion Square, the center of the city's business district.

PARISH GARDEN glowing with tulips *(right)* is tended by two nuns and a lay helper. The garden adjoins an 18th Century church on the Ile d'Orléans near Quebec.

IMMENSE VISTA of plowed fields and distant mountains seems to dwarf the cattle trotting from one pasture to another on a large farm near Lethbridge, Alberta.

SEA OF WHEAT surrounds Saskatchewan farmer R. S. Frisk as he examines his ripening grain. The Prairie provinces grow about 30 million acres of wheat each year.

SWEEPING PRAIRIES stretch almost

800 miles across Alberta and Saskatchewan to the foothills of the Rocky Mountains

PACIFIC PORT of Vancouver commands a spectacular site and serves as the shipping center of the West Coast

LARGE TIMBER RAFTS clog False Creek while waiting to be cut into lumber in Vancouver's sawmills. The city, its skyline dominated by several tall, modern buildings, ships lumber, fish and minerals from British Columbia and is also the western outlet for grain and oil from the Prairies. Growing fast since World War II, Vancouver today has about 900,000 people.

THE WILDERNESS of the North, while still largely undeveloped, challenges man's efforts to tame and explore it

LUXURIANT FORESTS roll down to the banks of the turbulent Peace River in northern British Columbia. Canada has vast tracts of virgin forest, enormous untapped sources of hydroelectric power and a wealth of undeveloped mineral deposits.

OCEAN OF ICE, a solid sheet mottled by snow, confronts the icebreaker *D'Iberville* as it plows through Norwegian Bay in the Queen Elizabeth Islands. Far northern Canadian waters, only a few hundred miles from the Pole, are frozen even in summer.

Completing the railroad that knit Canada into one nation, white-bearded Lord Strathcona, a Canadian Pacific official, drives the last

spike on November 7, 1885, at Craigellachie, British Columbia.

2

Plunder versus Settlement

THE plot is old as history, beloved by tellers of fairy tales and editors of boys' annuals. The king sends Boastful Harry and Quiet John into the enchanted forest on a dangerous mission. Boastful Harry returns first, reports that he has slain a dragon and is honored at court. Quiet John holds his peace and goes about his daily tasks. Time, and perhaps a woodcutter's beautiful daughter, unmask Harry and reveal the dragon-slayer as John. He inherits the kingdom and lives happily ever after.

Thus it was, and is, in Canada. For 700 years the Boastful Harrys of Europe sailed their ships across the Atlantic, gazed at the forbidding coastline, made small forays ashore and returned to the courts of their kings with wild tales of discovering Cathay, of great riches and strange adventures. The 10th Century Icelander Leif Eriksson was probably the first. The Italian John Cabot, in the employ of the English, so pleased them with his discovery of Newfoundland that they dubbed him "Great

Admiral," their rival to Columbus, and, as a contemporary observer noted, "vast honor is paid to him and he goes dressed in silk and these English run after him like mad."

France's Jacques Cartier, who in three voyages (1534, 1535, 1541) explored the Gulf of St. Lawrence and reached the site of what is now Montreal, inflamed his king with promises of "leaves of fine gold as thick as a mans nayle" and "stones like Diamants, the most faire, pollished and excellently cut that it is possible for a man to see." He brought back with him one of the first Canadians to visit Europe, an Indian chief named Donnacona, who cheerfully gave the French court what it wanted to hear in tales of "immense quantities of gold, rubies and other rich things," of "men who fly" and men who "have only one leg," and men who "never eat or digest."

OTHER explorers, Englishmen and Danes in search of a Northwest Passage to Asia, sailed their tiny ships past icebergs and through roaring currents into the broad inlets of northeastern Canada, often continuing for days in the belief that they were in open seas and not, as was the case, moving within an enormous strait. Henry Hudson drove his near-mutinous crew for more than a month of terrifying navigation through a strait which led to the huge bay that is named for him. In that vast dead end he moved like a man trapped in a maze until, at last, he beached his ship and waited out a dreadful winter. When spring came, he ordered his reluctant shipmates westward once more. Mutineers cast him and a handful of loyal companions into a shallop and turned the ship toward England. Most of the mutineers survived; the shallop did not.

The first example of the Quiet John type of hero, who came for treasure but stayed to settle the land, was Samuel de Champlain, the honest and good man who laid the foundations of the nation which is Canada. His journals, unlike those of earlier explorers, are filled with facts, not fantasies, for this remarkable Frenchman not only penetrated farther into the interior than any white man before him but was the first to see the country as a land where Frenchmen might live in peace and justice. This, in the year 1604, took more vision than we might now suppose. In that year, acting as "official recorder and geographer" of an expedition led by the Sieur de Monts, Champlain watched 35 out of a ship's company of 79 die in an effort to winter ashore on the island of Sainte Croix in the Bay of Fundy. Returning in 1608 as the leader of an expedition, he founded Quebec—and Canada—on the shores of the St. Lawrence River by building three small two-story buildings and a storehouse below the cliffs. Only eight out of 24 men survived that terrible winter.

But Champlain prevailed. He developed the fur trade in order to raise money for further exploration and colonization. He encouraged the Indians, among whom he had already proven himself in battle, to take young French boys to live with them and learn the wilderness skills. These boys became the famous *coureurs de bois* (forest runners), the vanguard of French exploration of the North American continent. He brought in missionaries and craftsmen. Even when his colony was starved out by British privateers and he and his men were shipped to Europe as British prisoners, his dream of colonization was not shaken and he returned in glory to the land which he called "New France." In 1634 he welcomed the first group of permanent colonists. One year later, old and stricken by paralysis, he died on Christmas Day in Quebec, the city he had founded.

CHAMPLAIN was New France and without him it is doubtful that French Canada would exist today. He was also the first to see that the chief obstacle to colonization was not the severe climate but "was on the part of the gentlemen of the Company [one of the French fur trading enterprises] who, to monopolize trade, did not even wish the country to be settled, and did not even wish to make the Indians sedentary." This antagonism between those

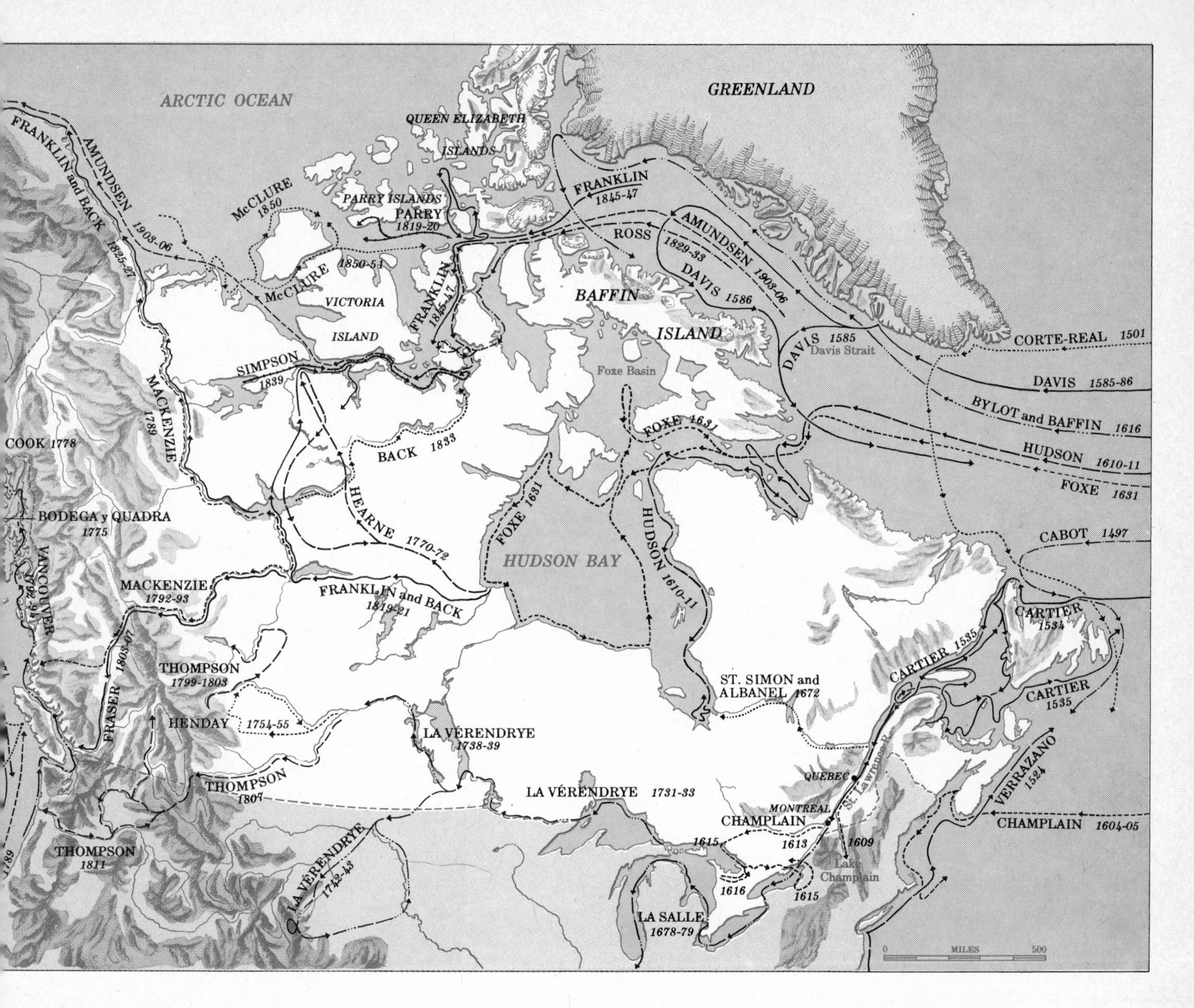

MEN WHO EXPLORED CANADA are set forth on the map above, together with the dates of their principal expeditions. The North American coastline was officially discovered in 1497 by the Genoese John Cabot, but the first man to penetrate the interior of the country was Jacques Cartier of France, who in 1534 explored the Gulf of St. Lawrence and in 1535 sailed 500 miles up the St. Lawrence River. Gaspar Corte-Real sailed along Newfoundland's coast. Samuel de Champlain was the chief founder of "New France" (mainly present-day Quebec) in the early 17th Century. Robert Cavelier, Sieur de LaSalle sailed the Great Lakes. An early prober of the northern seas was John Davis of England. Henry Hudson in 1610 discovered the bay which bears his name; the bay's western coast was finally charted in 1631 by Luke Foxe. Both Hudson and Foxe had set out to locate the Northwest Passage to Asia, as did William Baffin and Robert Bylot in 1616. Others who tried unsuccessfully during the next three centuries to find a viable passage included Sir John Franklin, who penetrated to the Alaskan coast; Sir George Back, who accompanied Franklin on all but his final voyage and also opened up a large area northwest of Hudson Bay; and Thomas Simpson, who discovered Victoria Island. Sir Robert McClure in 1850-1851 proved the existence of the passage, but the first successful crossing of the passage was only accomplished in 1903-1906 by the Norwegian Roald Amundsen. The Canadian West and the Rocky Mountain area were opened up by Sieur La Vérendrye, who also led an expedition into what is now the Dakota region of the U.S.; Sir Alexander Mackenzie, who achieved the first overland crossing to the Pacific; Captain George Vancouver, who circumnavigated Vancouver Island; David Thompson, who explored the upper Columbia River; Anthony Henday, the first to explore the plains of lower Saskatchewan and Alberta; and Simon Fraser. Canada's Pacific Coast was charted principally by a group of Spaniards, but the first European to land on the coast was Britain's Captain Cook.

who came to plunder Canada and the Quiet Johns who wished to make a home in the new country has echoed angrily in every phase of Canada's history.

Jesuits were among the missionaries Champlain brought in, and some of them tried to Christianize the Huron Indians and other tribes by living among them. They had little success. The Hurons would cheerfully be baptized 10 times a day for a glass of brandy, but their real preoccupations were the powerful Iroquois war bands who put villages to the torch, delighted in slaughter and once conducted a mock mass robed in the vestments of a murdered priest before the palisades of Montreal. In 1648 and 1649 the Iroquois finally wiped out the Huron villages, killing the heroic Jesuits in hideous tortures.

French military reinforcements routed the Iroquois with draconian efficiency. The Catholic Church grew, the fur trade prospered and more colonists were imported. The British, however, were awakening. In 1668 an English ship penetrated Hudson Strait and wintered at the mouth of the Rupert River. It returned to England with a promising cargo of furs. Two years later, England's Charles II issued a charter to "The Governor and Company of Adventurers of England trading into Hudson's Bay," a company which survives today as one of the most powerful business firms in Canada. A conflict was thus joined between English and French, part of the struggle for world dominance that raged through the 18th Century and ended only at Waterloo in 1815.

FRENCH explorers like La Salle, Marquette, Joliet and La Vérendrye ranged far into North America, the latter establishing a chain of fur-trading stations in the Canadian West. In the 1740s a French North American population which probably totaled less than 100,000 in all of the huge areas of Newfoundland, the region called Acadia (principally Nova Scotia), Quebec, and the Illinois and Louisiana territories had somehow managed to lay claim to a continent. This astonishing feat was possible only because the British settlers in America were not aware of their own strength. After years of friction culminating in the announcement of large territorial claims by the Ohio Land Company, chartered by the English in 1749, a North American war (the French and Indian War) broke out between Virginians and French Canadians.

This conflict became part of a larger conflict between English and French in Europe, the Seven Years' War (1756-1763). Before it ended, the British had finally vanquished the French in North America. After a bungling British start and brilliant generalship by the French leader Montcalm, the weight of numbers began to tell irrevocably against the French with the capture by the British in 1758 of Forts Frontenac, Duquesne and Louisbourg. In 1759 Fort Niagara fell and in that same year, with the defeat of Montcalm by Britain's General Wolfe, the dream of a French North America died where it had been born—in the small settlement founded by Samuel de Champlain under the cliffs of Quebec.

THE British set the pattern for the future of French Canada in the Quebec Act of 1774, which in effect reinstated the prewar status quo of French officialdom, substituting London for Versailles as the seat of power. This pleased the clergy and the ruling landowners but not the ordinary farmer, who, after 15 years of freedom following the surrender, was again obligated for tithes and other dues. However, in 1774, when the American Continental Congress, hoping to profit from the farmers' unrest, invited French Canadians to attend its meetings, it made the unfortunate mistake of asking them to help uphold English rights—meaning the rights of the English-speaking American settlers. The French Canadians, who regarded English-speaking settlers as enemies, were cold to the proposal and consequently the next year, when the American Revolution began, French Canadians sat on the fence.

The Revolution caused, as a side effect, the flight to Canada of thousands of British Loyalists who began to open up Upper Canada (now the province of Ontario), founded New Brunswick and instilled in Canadian minds a set of attitudes that, in diluted form, survive among the ruling classes of English descent today. These were: a rejection of Americans and the United States, a loyalty to Great Britain and a fondness for an aristocratic society of privilege in which they were the privileged group. This Loyalist immigration continued for a decade, but, in addition, thousands of other Americans crossed the border merely in search of a better home. According to a gazetteer of the period, "In 1812, more than 80 per cent of the population of Upper Canada was of American birth or descent, only a quarter of it Loyalist."

HOPES that some of these American settlers would turn against the British were voiced that same year when President James Madison launched an attack on Canada which was part of the larger conflict known to Americans as the War of 1812. But American Canadians had little sympathy with "Mr. Madison's War." Down in the Maritimes, the population made agreeable profits out of the sale of arms and privateering. Contraband trade with dissident New England groups made the war lucrative in Ontario and Quebec. English colonists, led by Britain's Sir Isaac Brock, imposed surrender on larger American forces at Detroit, while bands of French and English colonists joined to defeat the Americans at Lake Champlain.

While this was America's last open attempt to annex Canada, the United States would in the future support two prolonged guerrilla actions by Fenian raiders over the border, and for the next 150 years hotheaded American mavericks would try by threats, invitations and other devices to encourage the union of the two countries. Until this day, the War of 1812 has left its mark. J. B. Brebner, the leading historian of U.S.-Canadian relations, notes that this war, "more than any other single circumstance, nourished anti-Americanism as a basic element in . . . future Canadianism."

However, many Canadians could not help contrasting the colonial rule under which they lived with the stirring stories of new freedom in the United States. In 1837, inspired by Jacksonian democracy and angered by British refusal to grant certain French Canadian electoral rights, a gifted orator named Louis-Joseph Papineau openly threatened that French Canada would join the United States and led his rural supporters in rebellion against the Crown. Although American irregulars joined the rebels in battle, the revolt was ruthlessly suppressed. In the same remarkable year, English Canadians staged *their* one and only rebellion. Similarly inspired by American democracy and outraged by local injustices, a fiery, redheaded Scottish radical named William Lyon Mackenzie led a ragged group of Upper Canada settlers in revolt against the pro-British, urban, merchant class of the region. Again, American irregulars crossed the border to join the rebels. Again, the result was ignominious defeat.

True, in the eye of history, both Papineau and Mackenzie may seem inept and foolish amateurs. Their revolutions were the one ill-starred attempt at an uprising of the Quiet Johns, who had a stake in the Canadian land, against the Boastful Harrys, who saw it as a country to be plundered. It also is true that these ill-timed revolutions were secretly encouraged by the conservative masters of Canada, the better to crush them in their infancy. Yet the uprisings did not really fail. They alerted the British to the dangers of irresponsible government in these colonies and, eventually, led to the confederation of Canada.

CONFEDERATION, the union of four Canadian provinces—Nova Scotia, New Brunswick, Quebec and Ontario—into partial self-government, was carried out in 1867 by Sir John A. Macdonald, a bibulous, blarneying Tory who became the Canadian equivalent of George Washington. Sir John occupies a somewhat questionable position in Canadian history, for historians look askance at his sharp dealings, his drinking and his dissolute habits, at the same time that they admire his canny Scots statesmanship. He became prime minister of the newly confederated Canada, but it is generally considered that his success in building a Canadian Pacific Railway which would unite this huge country was his more lasting achievement.

For Confederation was pushed onto unwilling provincial governments both by English and Canadian financiers and railroad men who wanted to develop the West and by the British government, which was tired of defending a divided Canada against American attacks and saw Confederation as an answer. Even when the union was signed, however, the final power remained in London. The parliamentary model was British: At the head of the government was a British governor-general, the representative of the Crown; a Senate of 72 persons, nominated for life; and an elected House of Commons. Yet the idea of a federal government ruling over separate provincial governments came from the "hated" United States.

On November 7, 1885, the telegraph chattered across Canada. "The first train from Montreal is approaching Yale, within a few hours of the Pacific coast. On reaching the coast our running time from Montreal, exclusive of stoppages, will be five days, averaging twenty-four miles per hour." The transcontinental Canadian Pacific Railway was completed. Physically united at last, the huge area that the British, little more than 100 years before, had thought less valuable than the West Indian island of Guadeloupe developed probably the fastest growing economy on earth.

THE world began to bet heavily on Canada. Immense amounts of foreign capital—chiefly British and American—poured in for railroads, mines and factories. Hearing of the ready rail access to European markets, hundreds of thousands of Americans rushed across the border to farm Prairie wheatlands where, in one year, a good crop could make a man rich. The population jumped an astonishing 35 per cent in the decade from 1901 to 1911. With the introduction of efficient canning and refrigeration, fisheries revenues doubled. Railroad builders laying track near Cobalt, Ontario, uncovered slabs of almost solid silver. Strikes were made all along the line, not only of silver, but of gold, copper, zinc and other non-ferrous metals. It is not surprising that Sir Wilfrid Laurier, the first French Canadian to be elected premier of his country, announced at this time that "the 20th Century belongs to Canada."

Yet, in many ways, Canada was still a British colony. Even in matters of law, the final court of appeal was Britain's Privy Council. When

CANADA'S FIRST SETTLERS, THE INDIANS

When European explorers and colonists first began establishing settlements along the St. Lawrence, there were probably about 200,000 Indians in Canada. Early contacts were largely peaceful, despite some lurid outbreaks of fighting, and the Indians taught the white man how to make snowshoes and canoes, how to hunt moose and beaver, and how to raise and cook native vegetables like corn, squash and artichokes.

THE ERA OF THE FUR TRADERS

During the 19th Century the Indians, especially those tribes living on the Prairies, fell on evil times. Unscrupulous fur traders furnished the Indians with guns and encouraged them to wipe out the herds of buffalo on which these western Indians depended for food. The fur traders often paid the Indian hunters with cheap but potent rum. By 1900 a combination of disease, alcoholism and starvation had reduced the Indian population by half, to about 100,000.

THE SOLUTION: RESERVATIONS

The plight of the Indians prompted the government to establish reservations where it could provide food, shelter, medical care and schools and teach the Indians to grow wheat and raise cattle. There are more than 2,200 reserves in Canada, some very large and rich in good farmland, timber and minerals. Some Indian communities on the richer reservations hold property worth millions. Under government care, the Indians have made up their population loss, and by 1970 there will be about 230,000 of them in Canada.

TODAY'S OBJECTIVE: INTEGRATION

The reservations, although they probably saved many tribes from extinction, involve a kind of servitude, and the present government policy is to integrate all Indians into Canadian society. They may become citizens by renouncing "native" status and accepting the duties of ordinary citizens. Many Indian children now attend white schools, and more than 100 Indians attend Canadian universities. More and more Indians are turning from trapping and farming to industry, mining and lumbering.

Britain went to war in 1914 against Germany, the British government took it for granted that Canada was at war too. The assumption was justified. "Canadians," says A.R.M. Lower, "responded to the call as if they were building a new railroad." In the cruel emergency of war, Canada began to grow up. Canadians went overseas and discovered, among European strangers, that they were a nation, a separate American breed. Despite their tiny population, they lost as many men in combat as the United States, won 70 Victoria Crosses and rapidly lost their provincial awe of the mother country.

WHEN Britain's mighty Lord Kitchener calmly told Sir Sam Hughes, Canada's minister of militia, that the Canadian regiments newly arrived in Europe must be broken up among British regiments because "they are, of course, without training . . . and of very little use to us as they are," Hughes at once protested that this would kill recruiting in Canada. Kitchener looked coldly at the upstart colonial. "You have your orders, carry them out," he said. "I'll be damned if I will," Sir Sam replied, turned on his heel and marched away. The regiments stayed intact, and Canada, which began the war with one division under the command of a British general, ended it with four divisions under the command of a Canadian general. At war's end, Canada insisted on its right to sign the peace treaty and, shortly afterwards, applied for separate membership in the League of Nations.

World War I started Canada's industrialization. By 1920 the net value of manufactures surpassed that of agricultural production. The world—and most Canadians—did not realize this at the time. Canada still had less than nine million inhabitants and its enormous exports of wheat made the country seem simply a breadbasket, largely undeveloped and unexploited. But already then, as it does today, Canada's economic health closely followed the rise and fall of the U.S. economy, and this was particularly true in the West. Strikes and bitter labor disputes broke out, paralleling similar periods of labor unrest in the U.S. in the 1920s and early 1930s. When the Great Depression hit the United States, Canada went down for the count. The Prairie wheatlands went bankrupt. As world markets dropped, Canada, with a fourth of its national income dependent on exports, mainly of raw materials, was faced with a catastrophic fall in prices, and as soon as President Roosevelt announced his New Deal thousands of Canadians crossed the border, legally or illegally, in search of a better life. Canadian governments floundered in confusion and strange prophets rose with economic panaceas.

Even today the influence of the Depression is evident in the political life of the Canadian West. Two western provinces (Alberta and British Columbia) are run by the heirs of Social Credit, an evangelically tinged doctrine first propounded in Canada by William Aberhart, who was also head of the Prophetic Bible Institute of Alberta. Social Credit held that society's ills are mainly the result of insufficient purchasing power and proposed, among other measures, printing more money as a cure. And for 20 years, from 1944 to 1964, the Prairie province of Saskatchewan had North America's only socialist state government.

MEANWHILE, in one of those tiny, far-off foreign crises which make headlines only in the absence of news at home, Canada took a small but decisive step toward running its own affairs. In 1922 the British, engaged in putting down the Turks at Chanak in the international zone of the Dardanelles, summoned colonial governments to send troops. Canada's prime minister, Mackenzie King (see Chapter 1), brusquely announced that he could not provide troops without consulting the Canadian Parliament. It was a warning that Canadians would no longer underwrite British imperial policy.

Ever sensitive to diplomatic pressures, the British in 1931 granted Canada, together with several other former colonies, the status of an autonomous dominion within the Commonwealth in the Statute of Westminster. The statute also established the principle that Canadian legislation was no longer null and void if it conflicted with legislation passed by the parliament of Britain. Four years later, Britain's Privy Council relinquished its power as the final court of appeal in Canadian criminal cases.

Thus, at the outbreak of World War II, Canada was in the position of the eldest son who has been given his own front door key and has a job—but is still living in the family's house. Unlike the Americans or the Irish, Canadians had not fought for their independence. Their moves toward running their own affairs seem, in retrospect, the actions of a child testing a parent's will. Britain had long realized that Canada, the only dominion in the dollar, and not the sterling, currency block, and the only one bordering on a powerful English-speaking neighbor, would be difficult to hold onto should its citizens wish to break away. But Canada did not ask for freedom. Those who held power there continued to be bound by the old ties of sentimental attachment for Britain, by old fears and hatreds of the United States and by their desire to retain privileges founded on British rules of class and conduct.

Yet, in the years between the two world wars, a new and prickly nationalism was seeded. It was quite different from the nationalism of French Canadians who looked to the past as their moment of glory and wanted only to be left alone by the English-speaking majority. The new national feeling was born of the loneliness of people united in a huge and frightening country only by a railroad line—the nationalism of farming communities who had discovered in the valleys and prairies of Canada the only place they could call home.

IT stemmed also from the old antagonism of settler against merchant, but for the first time it included among its proponents a nucleus of educated Canadians—university professors, editors and civil servants—who made it into a quiet crusade. In 1919 Canada became the first British dominion to refuse to allow its citizens to accept British titles (earldoms, knighthoods, etc.). And in 1939, when Britain declared war on Germany, Canada was no longer automatically in. In fact, the country remained neutral until September 10, a week after the British entry. Then, with every Canadian party pledged against conscription and with many reservations as to what Canada's commitment should be, Canadians reluctantly went to war.

Canada, with the United States, became the arsenal of the Allied powers, and once again war raised the country to new levels of power and prestige. Canadians served in every theater of operations, fought with extreme gallantry and, as in 1914-1918, lost heavily in proportion to their numbers. When peace came, steel production had doubled, aluminum production had increased sixfold, new factories of every kind were in operation and American capital investment in Canada had hugely increased. Forest production had doubled in value, fisheries had tripled the value of their products and hydroelectric power had increased more than 40 per cent.

IN 1945 Canada emerged prosperous, powerful and indisputably a winner. Meanwhile, British power had severely declined and the United States was the new and uncontested leader of the West. Yet Canada did not become an American satellite. During the war Americans had become increasingly aware of Canadian skills and respectful of the country's claims as an independent nation. In 1949 the British colony of Newfoundland voted to join Confederation and become Canada's 10th province. Yet even with this addition of territory and manpower, Canada's strength came not from its size and population but from the productivity of the section of the economy that had been industrialized. It was still, in most areas, an undeveloped country and its total population was less than 14 million people. A new, heady boom began. Oil was discovered in the West, iron ore in Labrador and uranium in Ontario. Jobs went begging and immigrant ships jammed Canadian ports. It seemed that, at last, Sir Wilfrid Laurier's grandiloquent prediction had come true. The 20th Century *did* belong to Canada.

In a contemporary painting the fathers of Confederation are seen ending their task as Sir John A. Macdonald (center) rises to speak.

Hard Work and Statesmanship Making a Nation

The unification of Canada depended not just on politicians but also, like most things Canadian, on a conquest of the country's immense distances. Sir John A. Macdonald, aided by other able statesmen, engineered the Confederation of four Eastern provinces in 1867, and by 1871 the Western territories had joined the dominion. But true unification depended on the backbreaking labors of the track-laying gangs who, after four and a half years of battling blizzards and bogs and mountains, pushed the Canadian Pacific tracks all the way to the West Coast. In 1890 a flood of immigrants started flowing west, and spur lines began to bring out the produce of new farms and mines. Only then did Canada become, in truth, a nation. But still it took skillful politicians to keep the nation unified, to guide it through economic depressions and two world wars and to chart a course into the troubled mid-century.

Joyous crowds in the already busy port of Vancouver welcome the arrival in May 1887 of the first train to the city from the East.

MAKESHIFT OFFICE of a land agent named Horne is set up to sell lots to the immigrants who followed the railroad west *(left)*. The Canadian Pacific, granted 25 million acres, sold many at $2.50 an acre.

MERCANTILE LINK is established at a siding in Calgary *(opposite)* as railroad freight cars take on a load of Hudson's Bay Company furs brought from Edmonton in old-fashioned two-wheeled carts.

OPENING THE WEST, the railroad linked together older means of transport

Hudson's Bay laborers haul supply boats up the Athabaska River. "The Bay" forged many trade routes before the railroad was built.

FIRST PRIME MINISTER of the nation he helped unite, Sir John A. Macdonald, who was born in Glasgow, showed his Scots tenacity as he drove the Canadian Pacific to completion.

IDEALISTIC POLITICIAN and first French prime minister (1896-1911), Sir Wilfrid Laurier *(below)* worked to reconcile French and English Canada and to develop the nation's trade.

SKILLFUL NEGOTIATOR who was prime minister for more than 21 years, W. L. Mackenzie King helped keep Canada united during World War II despite a controversy over conscription.

POLITICAL LEADERS have brought unusual stores of vigor and wisdom to the task of guiding the nation

POSTWAR MODERATE, Louis St. Laurent, the second French Canadian to become prime minister, presided over the country's boom in the prosperous years that followed World War II.

SUCCESSFUL DIPLOMAT Lester B. Pearson, 14th prime minister, restored confidence in Canada abroad and was awarded the Nobel Peace Prize for work at the United Nations.

REVERED GOVERNOR-GENERAL, Vincent Massey was the first Canadian appointed to the country's highest honorary post. His most noted achievement was the Massey Report on the arts.

Arms raised in victory, Pierre Elliott Trudeau acknowledges cheers from his supporters on April 6, 1968, as he learns he has been elected

the Liberal party's leader and made Canada's prime minister.

3

A Renewed Confidence

AN immigrant arriving in Canada in the early 1950s felt much as would an immigrant arriving in the United States in the hectic boom years of the Roaring Twenties. The atmosphere was one of intense excitement; a feeling was abroad that old customs and institutions were dying by the hour; a consciousness of the country's new power and status among nations was everywhere apparent. The talk of ordinary citizens touched on rumors of great new fortunes being made. Manners were egalitarian yet somehow ruthless. At any moment anyone—or everyone—might become rich.

If the immigrant arrived in winter, he encountered a cold such as he had probably never known and walked through streets filled with the brown-sugar slush of snow that had been trampled on by thousands of passersby. If he arrived in summer, he met an unexpected heat, dry, dusty, intense—the baking temperature of a huge continent. The cities split at their extremities, disgorging long, untidy entrails of new concrete factories, shopping centers and suburban office blocks. In Montreal, ancient streetcars were shuffled off to junkyards and replaced by bright new buses. In Toronto a shiny new subway line was opened. In both cities, the old webs of overhead street wiring were being torn down. Underpasses and thruways were being built. Faded English tearooms were being reborn as *espresso* bars, and German delicatessens replaced flyblown corner groceries. And, everywhere, there was talk of huge foreign investment and of new, bold schemes for industrial development.

WEST COAST boosters told of the Swedish magnate who had rented one tenth of British Columbia for exploration and development. There were newspaper stories of the U.S.-Canadian find of oil and natural gas in Alberta which would shortly turn that province into a new Texas. There were rumors that the German steelmaster Krupp had moved into the Ungava iron fields in northern Quebec and that Rothschild money was pouring into Labrador. In Quebec, American interests had turned up the world's largest titanium deposit.

The new bright lights of the cities made the surrounding wilderness seem even more lonely. Rural settlers crowded into the towns and premium wages were offered to people willing to work in the undeveloped areas of the North. The government announced that 61 per cent of the population had become urban. But if, even in the cities, the new wave of immigrants mourned the lack of theater, concerts and art shows and of the café life of the lands they had left, they were sincerely assured by their new compatriots that all this was on the way. There was, in the decade of 1947 to 1957, a feeling abroad in Canada that nothing was impossible, that everyone's dream was on the point of fruition. Newspapers informed Canadians that they were the world's largest per capita importers, and, for a time, this new country became the fourth largest trading nation on earth.

That same decade was the Augustan age of Canadian business. It was an age when the most powerful man in government was the minister of trade and commerce, a tough, brilliant, former American named Clarence Decatur Howe, who ran 21 government-controlled companies and government committees as though they were branches of General Motors, regarded Parliament as a nuisance and, if challenged there, would ask, "Who's going to stop us?" Under his suzerainty, American, British, Swiss, German and Swedish interests were wheeled and dealt into large shares in Canada's industrial expansion program. If, in this golden age, it sometimes might have seemed to the immigrant that mining czars and department-store magnates stood higher in the public esteem than statesmen or scholars, Canadians would rebut the charge by citing their pride in Canada's record at the United Nations. There, in the postwar years, and particularly in 1955 and 1956, the country made world headlines as mediator in disputes involving both Great Powers and newly emergent nations.

IN fact, had the United Nations not existed, it might have been invented by Canada. Canadians are a committee-minded people who have long favored the British method of handling tricky or complex issues by setting up a royal commission of experts to study the problem at hand and come up with a set of recommendations. Although critics of this system complain that it is simply a convenient way of putting important and pressing problems on the shelf, it is true that, in Canada, such commissions have usually been served by able and dedicated men whose recommendations have been responsible for some of the major reforms enacted into law. In addition, Canadians have always favored a strong career civil service and the creation of a corps of career diplomats, patterned on the British model.

It is not surprising, therefore, that in the 1950s, as now, Canadians moved with ease in the committee rooms and corridors of the U.N. building in New York. In 1955, the U.N. admitted 16 new nations, largely as a result of a skillful campaign conducted by Paul Martin, chairman of the Canadian delegation to the Assembly. And in 1956, when Western unity and the U.N itself were jointly threatened by the British-French attack on the Suez Canal, a resolution drafted by Canada's then foreign minister, Lester B. Pearson, brought U.N. forces to intervene, defeated the Franco-British power bid, ended the crisis and, a year later, won for Mr. Pearson, and Canada, the Nobel Peace Prize.

Suez, for Canadians, was a decisive showdown, an irrevocable choosing of sides. British Tories, making a grandstand play to regain for their country the status of a Great Power, had tried the old Imperial strategy of sending in gunboats to intimidate the natives. The senior "white" dominions were, naturally, expected to go along with the decision. Australia and New Zealand backed Britain. Canada, however, backed the United Nations. While Canada's action was influenced less by Washington than by the respect which Prime Minister Louis St. Laurent had for the neutralist views of India's Prime Minister Nehru, who deplored such colonial actions by the Great Powers, it was nevertheless true that, in backing the United Nations against the mother country of Britain, Canada seemed to be siding, for once, with the "hated" United States.

YET, surprisingly, the decision caused little public outcry. True, the Canadian Conservative party censured the government in Parliament, supported the British action and attacked President Eisenhower's support of the United Nations position as "unrealistic." But the Liberal party's St. Laurent, the second French Canadian to become prime minister of his country, echoed the feelings of most Canadians when he angrily told Parliament: "The era when the supermen of Europe could govern the whole world is coming pretty close to an end." He was speaking not of Adolf Hitler but of Britain's Sir Anthony Eden.

There were other meaningful signs of Canada's changing position. As late as 1940, Canada and the U.S. had no official channel for military cooperation in the event of an attack on the North American continent. Now, with Canada as the northern buffer between the U.S. and Russia, three lines of defense against attack over the North Pole were going up on Canadian territory: the Pinetree Line, operated jointly by Americans and Canadians, a tracking, warning and intercepting force stretching from the Atlantic to the Pacific; the Mid-Canada Line, an unmanned chain of radar warning stations built solely by Canada; and the DEW (Distant Early Warning) Line, built by the United States across the Canadian Arctic wilds at a cost of more than $700 million U.S. The sight of U.S. soldiers posted under "Keep Out" signs on Canadian soil did, at first, stir old fears and misgivings about loss of Canadian sovereignty. Today, in an age of increasing "nuclear sophistication," many Canadians believe, rightly or wrongly, that these warning lines are fast becoming obsolete. This belief is not shared, it would seem, by the U.S. and Canadian defense commands. The lines remain operational.

In the 1950s also, Canada got its first native-born governor-general, officially the representative of the British Crown and as such the highest dignitary in the land. Previously, the post had largely been a retirement plum for well-connected English noblemen and over-aged generals. Vincent Massey (a brother of the actor Raymond Massey and a member of the Massey-Ferguson farm-equipment dynasty) was governor-general from 1952 until 1959. A frail, physically unimposing but highly intelligent man, Massey traveled into areas of Canada

THE DOLLAR, CANADIAN & U.S.

For most of the 1950s, Canada's dollar was worth slightly more than the U.S. dollar. Allowed to fluctuate in the exchange market by a special arrangement with the International Monetary Fund, it rose to a peak value of $1.06 U.S. in 1957. Later it dropped, and in 1962 economic pressures forced Canada to peg it at 92½ cents U.S.—and thereby to stop the fluctuations. For the sake of convenience, all dollar figures in this volume, unless otherwise noted, are given in terms of the Canadian dollar.

never before visited by a governor-general, emphasized at all times his Canadian birth, warned Canada's business-minded power elite that culture outlasts capital gains and was perhaps the best governor-general the country had ever had. Steeped in British tradition, he had tried to bring the Crown closer to the Canadian people. But when he died late in 1967, a new nation and a new society were slowly being born, and his casket was wrapped not in the Red Ensign with the Union Jack in one corner but in the new Canadian red maple leaf flag.

After Massey's retirement in 1959, the job of governor-general had been given for the first time to a French Canadian and Roman Catholic, General Georges Philias Vanier. Vanier proudly declared, "We *have* a Canadian identity," and he deplored those "who say that Canadians are a rudderless people." In 1967, the old general—he had helped found Quebec's famed Royal 22nd Regiment in 1914—died in office. His successor as Governor-General, Daniel Roland Michener, fluently bilingual and scholarly, won the approval of even those antimonarchist Canadians who hoped he might be Canada's last governor-general.

IN the postwar boom years, which began in 1947 and came to an end 10 years later, Ottawa was the capital of the second most-favored economy on earth. Canadians, to their surprise, found themselves making gifts and loans to foreign countries, lowering tariffs and cutting red tape on imports, much in the manner of a junior America engaged in its own Marshall Plan. In Canada itself vast projects were completed. Two great pipeline systems were built to deliver Prairie crude oil to Ontario and the Pacific Coast. The St. Lawrence Seaway, long a U.S.-Canadian dream, was put under construction. Canadians, flushed with new confidence, voted to build the seaway alone when U.S. Congressional delays threatened to kill the project. Later, the Americans reversed their decision and joined in.

In the boom years of the early 1950s, few Canadians worried that much of their new-found wealth was a result of foreign investment which, in changed circumstances, might be reduced or partially withdrawn. The government, busily engaged in luring new foreign customers, did little planning for the long-range future. Pockets of unemployment were largely ignored. Inflation and the wage spiral were words not mentioned in polite government and business circles. But in other parts of the world economists and financiers, worried by this "look-Ma-no-hands" attitude toward the future, began to hedge their bets. By 1957 the roulette wheel of Canadian prosperity had reversed its spin. The ball began dropping in other slots.

NO one cause produced Canada's new difficulties. But in 1957, like a gambler in a bad run of luck, the nation began to lose on several bets at once. The boom had pushed wages to a level second only to the U.S. But, unlike the U.S., Canada has a small population, and even in a mild recession it could not absorb these costs. Small production runs and a multiplicity of Canadian concerns competing against each other weakened the country's industries. For example: in 1961, 10 Canadian factories produced a total of 240,500 refrigerators, but U.S. factories had an average annual output of 275,000 each. Naturally, it was hard for Canadian firms in these circumstances to keep their production costs at competitive levels. The refrigerator manufacturers have, in fact, managed to market products which compare in price with American models, but the problem remains acute in many of Canada's industries.

Canadian provincial governments had spent heavily on social and public works programs. The nation had borrowed foreign capital for expansion projects faster than the Treasury could pay it off. After 1955 the foreign balance-of-payments deficit increased from $400 million to a billion dollars annually. European investment was shifting away from Canada to back a busy and prosperous Europe, and Americans could not be expected to increase their stake in the country at the spectacular rate they had maintained since 1945.

Yet in November of 1957, when the downturn had been operating for several months, few Canadians seemed aware that the country might face a serious recession.

Economic difficulties were not a major campaign issue in the spring of 1957 when the Liberal government fell to the Conservatives after 22 years of unbroken rule. American domination of Canada's economy *was* a campaign issue, mostly as a play on English Canadian fears of U.S. interference and in an appeal to pro-British sentiment. But the main issues were autocratic Liberal rule and the government's failure to reduce taxes. The Conservatives, led by John G. Diefenbaker, a rangy Prairie lawyer with a Bible-punching platform manner, won mainly because the voters wanted a change.

Elected, Diefenbaker made an emotional appeal to Britain to increase its trade with Canada. His aim was to switch 15 per cent of Canadian trade away from the U.S. toward Britain. The British politely allowed that this was a pleasant thought and offered a plan for a free-trade area. However, having made headlines at home and abroad, Diefenbaker did not pursue the matter further and, a few months later, fell back on his predecessors' policy of encouraging American investment.

BUT by 1960 Canada's economy, closely tied to that of the United States, was reflecting a U.S. recession. Unemployment in Canada rose to 7.2 per cent of the labor force. The Canadian dollar, once floating freely at about $1.06 in U.S. money, kept slipping in value and was, at last, realistically pegged by the Canadian government at 92½ U.S. cents. The Maritime provinces, traditionally the depressed section of the Canadian economy, were existing largely on federal subsidies and federal building projects. Corporate profits declined sharply. In the ensuing alarm, many Canadians looked anxiously for a scapegoat. The latent anti-Americanism long present in the Canadian consciousness had been simmering since the early 1950s when Canadians were appalled at the hysteria stirred up in the U.S. by Senator McCarthy. It had grown stronger during the political campaign of 1957, when Diefenbaker repeatedly denounced American domination of Canadian industry. And so, in 1960, Left and Right in Canada for once found common cause.

Canada's economic ills were now blamed on American investment, which had curbed the country's independence and which (mysteriously) was frustrating efforts to put the economy back in working order. Everyone must unite to keep the American wolf from the door. Economists announced that 69 per cent of Canada's petroleum industry, 53 per cent of its mining and smelting industry and almost half of its manufacturing were now controlled by Americans. Businessmen complained that the U.S. companies operating in Canada refused to hire Canadian executives. These subsidiary companies, they said, relied for research and technological advance on the U.S. parent companies, thus robbing Canadians of jobs, and then further sabotaged the Canadian economy by refusing to compete in export markets with the parent company. Trade union leaders charged that American companies maintained a double wage standard for Canadian and American employees.

Many of these complaints had been heard before and some were justified. But the Canadians themselves were not blameless in the question of foreign control of their industries. Many of them had placed their investment capital not in Canadian projects but in Texas oil, Brazilian traction, Gold Coast power plants and other foreign enterprises which promised quicker and more profitable returns. And if American investment were to be removed from Canada, what would take its place?

BUT even at the height of anti-American feeling in the early 1960s, ordinary Canadians suspected that something more than anti-American oratory would be needed to solve Canada's economic problems. And Canada's more far-sighted business leaders pointed out that anti-American political attitudes would worsen, not improve, the citizen's economic lot.

A Renewed Confidence

Thus gradually a sort of grass roots *Realpolitik* took hold of the country. The people no longer seemed to believe in the excuses of their leaders, and in the 1962 federal elections they produced what amounted to a vote of no-confidence in all four major parties. And in 1963, when they again repeated this vote pattern, they proved that the veiled anti-American campaign waged by Tory John Diefenbaker was no longer a vote-getting device. In electing a Liberal government led by Lester B. Pearson, a government committed to maintain Canada's defense commitments, the electorate again rejected an anti-American orientation.

For most of Pearson's stewardship, there was even less reason for such an orientation. Despite an uneasy beginning, Pearson in his five years as prime minister managed to accomplish an extraordinary amount; although he never was lucky enough to have a parliamentary majority, he managed to make good his promise to govern as if he had one. He brought through more legislation than any previous government in Canadian history, making particular gains in social welfare. He unified the armed services and achieved divorce reform that had been thought impossible for a century. But his most substantial contribution was to national unity and the symbols of national identity. In 1964 he gambled that Canadians were ready for a flag of their own—and he won. At the same time he took steps to awaken his own party and English Canada to the urgent need to make some adjustment to Quebec's growing demand for greater recognition *(Chapter 6)*, and toward this end he began the first steps toward long overdue constitutional reform that would begin to make Canada for the first time truly bilingual and bicultural.

THE HARD-WORKING BEAVER

Ever since the trade in beaver furs played a great role in the opening up of Canada, beavers have been

a symbol of Canadian industriousness and well-being. A number of fortunes were made in furs, and beaver hats long were fashionable in Europe as marks of status. For a time beaver skins were accepted as currency in Canada; later, special beaver coins were issued. Even today the animal appears on Canada's five cent piece *(above)*.

Throughout he maintained his jaunty, casual, cheerful demeanor—which was deceptive because Lester Pearson was essentially a subtle and complicated man. In all his dealings he made the best use of his skills as a diplomat. Said one observer, "Had any other man been in power from 1963 on, any man less flexible than Pearson showed himself to be, the country might have been fractured. He managed to retain federal authority, and kept his cool."

With the Pearson accomplishments came a new wave of prosperity. The post-World War II investment in manufacturing was beginning to pay off, and exports rose. Business boomed in the mid-1960s. The gross national product increased by 67 per cent between 1961 and 1967, and wages rose by a third while prices were rising less than one fifth; almost 1.5 million new jobs were created. Canada was selling huge amounts of wheat to both the Soviet Union and China, the largest sale being an $800 million shipment to the U.S.S.R. in 1966. The upsurge lasted until 1967—and then it petered out. Suddenly profits dropped, prices began catching up to wages, and there was danger of inflation. Unemployment grew.

As had happened before, bad times in Canada brought back bad feeling toward the United States. Much of the impetus for the boom of the 1960s had been supplied by investment and initiative from the U.S., and now the fall-off in the boom rekindled resentment against U.S. economic overlordship. The statistics were alarming: in the manufacturing, petroleum, natural gas, mining and smelting industries combined, American ownership by 1968 was up to 80 per cent.

Once again, a number of solutions were suggested. One was economic union with the U.S., a step that had previously been outlined by *Maclean's* magazine, a sort of Canadian *Saturday Evening Post,* which often reflects English Canadian middle-class thinking. "Canada can prosper as a junior partner with the U.S. in a continental economic region, with predominantly north-south trading lines," the magazine stated. It went on to say, "Unless we find the courage for this kind of gamble, Canada faces the alternative of becoming a sort of Manchuria-with-hockey-players, supplying raw materials for others to process while our standard of living slides ever lower."

A still stronger viewpoint was propounded by Professor Harry G. Johnson, a Canadian economist. Johnson has informed startled audiences in Canada that "the choice is between resisting the trend toward closer integration with the United States, and making a definite move to confirm and accelerate it. Economically," he says, "the arguments for integration with the United States are overwhelming."

Overwhelming they may be, but Canadian governments will continue to fight them. Even Lester Pearson's Liberal government, which came into power partly on pledges to improve U.S.-Canadian relations, had proposed a set of drastic new taxes aimed at checking U.S. control of Canada's industries. The most stringent proposal was shamefacedly withdrawn within a few days of its announcement, following strong protests by the Canadian financial community and swift declines on the Montreal and Toronto stock exchanges. But few official voices were heard attacking the anti-American principle involved in imposing it.

SO persistent was the outcry against U.S. involvement that in 1967 the Pearson government authorized a high-level, comprehensive study of foreign investment in Canada. The study, made under the leadership of Privy Council President Walter Gordon, resulted in the so-called Watkins Report, a mammoth document named after the head of the task force of economists who made the inquiry. Gordon's reputation for having long advocated "buying back" Canada from the Americans had led many observers to expect the Report to recommend curbing U.S. investment, but it surprised them. Far from cutting back on American investing, the Report said, Canada should welcome it.

The real issue, said the panelists, was "not whether foreign investment is worthwhile, but rather how to increase its benefits and decrease its costs." The most worrisome cost was plainly the extraterritorial application of U.S. law. "The intrusion of American law and policy into Canada by the medium of a Canadian subsidiary," they wrote, "erodes Canadian sovereignty and diminishes Canadian independence." Particularly irritating were U.S. controls on how subsidiary companies invest their funds and U.S. pressures against trading with Communist countries like China. To guard against such controls the Report advised setting up "countervailing" powers to buttress Canadian economic independence. A key recommendation was that groups of investors—both domestic and foreign—be organized to embark on new risk ventures, a spirit that has been all too lacking in Canada until now.

PROVOCATIVE and controversial, the Report was not immediately accepted by Pearson's government. But it would provide the basis for significant future debate, and above all it represented the new mood of realism in Canada. That mood was if anything heightened by the arrival of Pierre Elliott Trudeau to power in the spring of 1968 as Pearson's successor. Endorsing the main recommendation of the Watkins Report, Trudeau argued that the best way for Canadians to protect their independence was to work harder and take more risks on their own behalf. In a dramatic new departure he also announced that the country should reconsider its entire foreign policy and defense commitments, with an eye to pulling back its forces wherever they seemed no longer useful from Canada's point of view. Canadians might well feel that, after the many stresses of the past, a new door was opening.

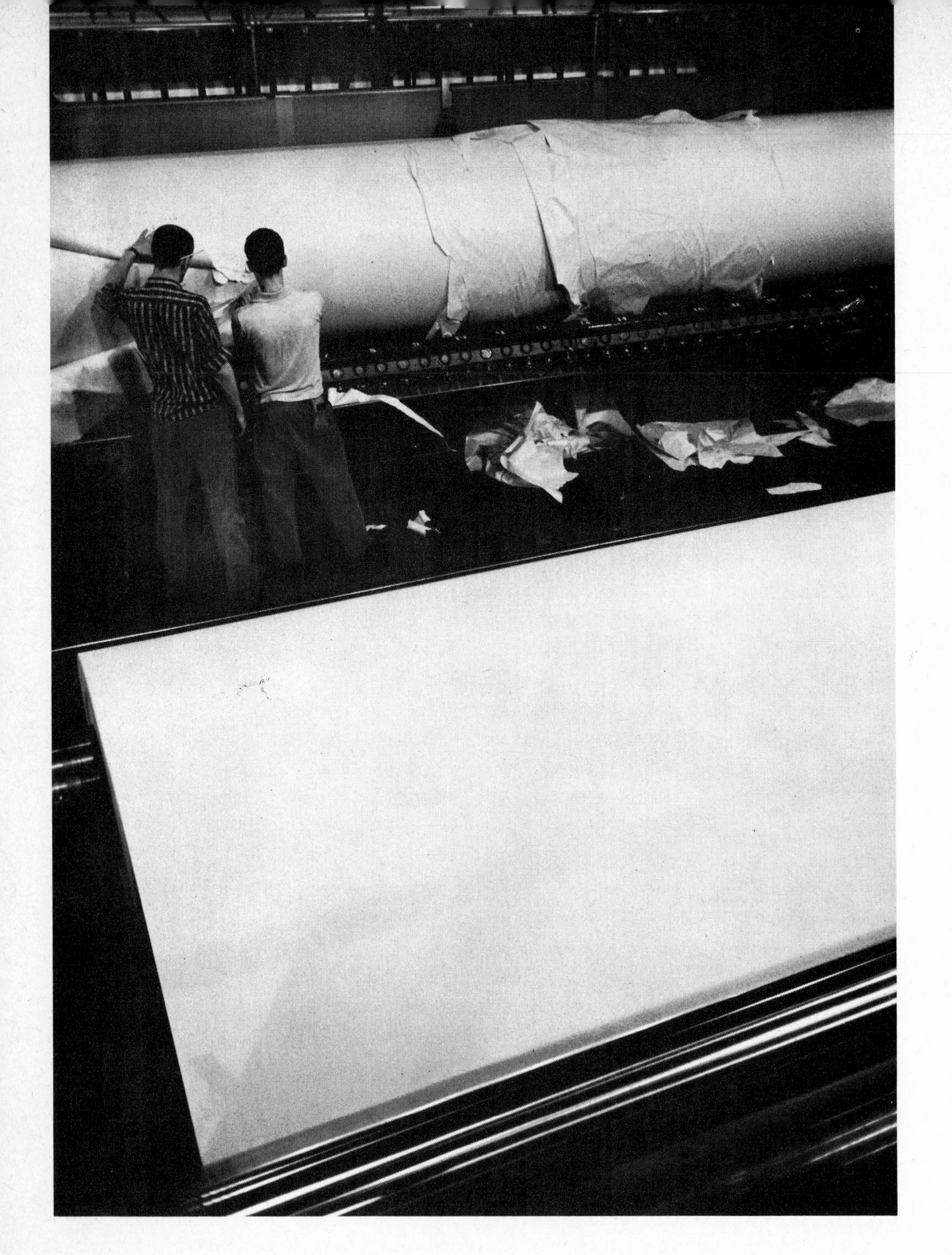

PAPERWORKERS strip unevenly rolled newsprint from a giant drum *(left)* in a mill at Baie Comeau, Quebec. Canada manufactures 40 per cent of the world's newsprint.

LOGROLLERS load barked logs *(right)* into barges outside a Baie Comeau mill. These logs will be shipped up the St. Lawrence to one of Ontario's numerous paper mills.

Enlarging Old Industries and Forging New Ones

Canada has one of the world's wealthiest economies. Its pulp and paper industries have long led the world. More recently enormous expansion has occurred in the smelting of various metals, and quantities of oil and natural gas have been found near the Prairie wheatlands. But, paradoxically, Canada's economic growth has been held in check by the country's very assets: its size and richness. The distances that the products of mine and mill must travel have involved crippling costs and may hinder the exploitation of remote regions for years to come.

BOLD PROJECT to build an aluminum plant at Kitimat in British Columbia involved great feats of engineering

SKILLED RIGGERS prepare to string a high-tension electric cable to a tall aluminum tower *(left)*. Cables were strung across 42 miles of rugged mountain country to bring power from hydroelectric generators to the plant at Kitimat.

STACKED INGOTS of aluminum await shipment in the railroad yard at Kitimat. To get power for the Kitimat smelters a huge dam was constructed, an entire river system was rerouted and giant generators were built inside a mountain.

BIS

NEW STORAGE TANKS at Sarnia, Ontario, mark the end of a pipeline that carries crude oil east from the Prairies. Another pipeline carries the refined product from Sarnia to Toronto.

OIL REFINING expands

REFINERY ENGINEERS study charts of the Imperial Oil Company's plant at Sarnia *(right)*. Processing about 1,174,000 barrels a day, Canada's refinery industry is the world's ninth largest.

HUGE CRACKING PLANT at Sarnia helps supply nearby "Chemical Valley," Canada's largest group of petrochemical units. Canadian refining has increased 400 per cent in 20 years.

rapidly as new plants and pipelines are built to handle the output of Prairie wells

DARING SCHEMES to discover and exploit Canada's natural wealth are being undertaken with increasing frequency

ARCTIC OIL WELL, part of an expedition backed by 17 U.S., Canadian and British petroleum companies to find oil in the far north, is reflected in the ice of a nearby lake. The islands of Canada's Arctic may hold oil reserves rivaling the Middle East's.

LONGEST PIPELINE in Canada, which now carries natural gas 2,145 miles from western Saskatchewan to Montreal, inches its way toward Swift Current Creek during its construction in 1956. Four spur lines carry gas across the border into the U.S.

TORONTO with its banks, offices and stock exchange is a nerve center for the country's growing industry

SOBERLY DRESSED BUSINESSMEN, seated in comfortable leather chairs, lunch in the quietly elegant dining room of Toronto's Board of Trade in the center of the city's financial area.

STOCK-EXCHANGE FLOOR bustles with activity as brokers watch stock prices flash on the trading posts. The board on the wall informs them when their offices have an order to place.

8 8 8

Students and professors, wearing academic gowns, mingle over coffee on a porch of Trinity College, one of the eight colleges that make

up the Faculty of Arts and Sciences at the University of Toronto.

4

Through the Looking Glass

FOR both Frenchmen and Americans Canada has the eerie fascination of what might have been. It appears to be a land where history stopped. To the visiting Frenchman, the province of Quebec offers a glimpse of a France unchanged by the fall of the Bastille, a France which continues to hold many beliefs that predate the age of *Liberté, Egalité, Fraternité* and the five French republics which followed it. To Americans, English Canada is America as it might have remained had there been no War of Independence.

Thus, an American crossing the border experiences an odd sensation. These people seem much like himself, but there is a foreign patina to the landscape. In the customs shed a large colored photograph of Queen Elizabeth is displayed. Bejeweled and wearing a tiara, she sits as majestic as Britannia, smiling with the game uncertainty of a Royal Personage trying to unbend. And, when our traveler leaves customs and drives along his first Canadian highway, he will notice that some of the Fords and Chevrolets on the road seem slightly different from the cars back home. They are. They have different trade names, color schemes and occasionally different trim to conform with Canadian tastes. At the first railroad crossing he comes to, he sees the usual sequence of diesel engine, flatcars, gondolas and caboose rush past, the engineer sounding his horn. What could be more like home? Later he may learn that the railroad, the Canadian National (the longest rail system in North America), is owned lock, stock and branch line by the government of Canada.

AS our traveler enters the outskirts of his first Canadian town, he feels even less at home. Those soldiers wear British-style uniforms. Flying over a motor court, next to the flag of one of the Canadian provinces, is the recently adopted Canadian national emblem—a red ensign bearing in the center a white field with a single red maple leaf. That crocodile of leggy schoolgirls in black stockings and crested blazers seems to have strayed off an English country lane. The mailboxes are emblazoned with the monogram "EIIR" and a crown. The dollar he receives in change faintly resembles his own but, on inspection, carries a picture of the Queen and announces its denomination in both English and French. If, in any major Canadian city, he asks to be directed to the best hotel, he may well be sent to a hotel owned either by the Canadian National Railway, and therefore by the government, or by the Canadian Pacific Railway, which got its start largely through government subsidy. He will discover that the government owns an airline, but that there is also a major private airline—and that this pattern of government and private enterprise existing side by side is accepted as the norm by Canadians.

The department stores, the restaurants, the food, the supermarkets—all remind him of home. Yet there continue to be small differences. He may be given tea instead of coffee. The cigarettes on sale look and taste like English cigarettes. Taxi drivers call him "sir."

The French traveler may also begin by experiencing the same odd mixture of familiarity and foreignness. He will be fascinated by the old-fashioned provincial French still spoken in Quebec and, seeing the crowded churches and the extent of the clergy's influence and holdings, may be tempted to imagine that he is in a France before the Terror. He will find French books and magazines on every bookstall; he will eat French cooking and will even watch French-speaking television. But, sooner or later, he will conclude that these people are different. Camille Anbert, a writer for the French magazine *Réalités*, found that the French Canadians of Quebec province seem almost completely Americanized to the Frenchman from France. He was surprised to find that even their shrines show American influence. "At the Oratory of Saint Joseph [in Montreal] . . . the 'Ladies' and 'Gentlemen' are situated in the edifice itself, only two steps from the nave, and four . . . escalators . . . propel the pilgrims toward five showcases where they can venerate a lifesized wax effigy of the founder, Brother André, and also, in a box made of red glass, his heart suspended from a thread."

What astonished M. Anbert was not the sight of wax effigies and pickled hearts, which belong to the European tradition of such places of pilgrimage, but the American efficiency of well-run plumbing facilities *within* the church, the showcases, the escalators and the astonishingly varied range of services—including a gift shop run on supermarket principles—which make Saint Joseph's Oratory a uniquely North American shrine.

LIKE Lewis Carroll's Alice, both M. Anbert and the American visitor have peered through the looking glass and seen that, in this landscape that mirrors many aspects of their own, "things go the other way." For history does not stop. It merely takes another turning. The American Revolution turned English Canada into a poor relation, frequently snubbed by Britain during British attempts to placate a powerful new United States. The French Revolution terrified the clergy and officials of Quebec, causing them to cut the umbilical cord with the mother country, leaving the French Canadians embittered and alone. Both French and English Canada have, therefore, grown up feeling neglected. "Canadians," says Professor A.R.M. Lower, "are the children of divorced parents and they know the bitterness that comes of a broken home. . . ."

BOTH have watched America's exhilarating rise to its present position as one of the most envied and imitated countries in the world with the confused emotions of the less fortunate—with admiration and envy, with a desire to imitate coupled with a fear of losing their own identities. Thus, while both have borrowed from their parent countries, they have come more and more to adopt the manners and attitudes of their successful, envied sister—America. They have learned to transform some of their borrowings, making them peculiarly their own, and to reject those American ways which do not please them.

Their problem—living with, and assimilating, the influence of American popular culture—was until recently purely a local one. But today, what has happened in Canada is happening all over the world. Thai villagers watch American Westerns. Paris restaurants serve hamburgers. Londoners shop in supermarkets. German *Halbstarke* youth dress like Marlon Brando, Russian *stilyagi* dig Benny Goodman, Latin Americans play *beisbol,* sheiks drink 7-Up and Ghanaians drive Oldsmobiles. And all this has happened by osmosis: it is, simply, a kind of entertainment, a way of living, a set of tastes which seem to suit the second half of the 20th Century. To the rest of the world, now facing the first bout of this infection, Canada presents an interesting case history.

Take the movies. Canadian production of feature films is occasional and small, and so the bulk of Canada's movie fare comes from Hollywood. British films are shown principally in the larger cities. French films run mostly in Quebec. But, unlike Asian and European audiences, Canadians can distinguish what is fact from what is fantasy in Hollywood's image of the United States. They should know. Americans and Canadians both make roughly 30 million crossings of the border into each other's countries every year. In addition, a surprising number of Canadians have helped to create Hollywood's dream images. Louis B. Mayer, once the shah-in-shah of Metro-Goldwyn-Mayer, grew up in Saint John, New Brunswick. Mary Pickford, the original "America's Sweetheart," was a Toronto girl. Marie Dressler, Norma Shearer, Walter Huston, Raymond Massey, Walter Pidgeon, Glenn Ford and other such seemingly all-American idols were, in reality, Canadians passing as Yanks. On their home ground, Canadians have wisely resisted the urge to compete with Hollywood, but the government-sponsored National Film Board produces documentary films that have won awards all over the world.

JAZZ has been part of Canadian life ever since Prohibition sent trainloads of Americans north of the border in search of a drink. Montreal bloomed as the "Paris of North America," and its nightclubs featured American jazz musicians waiting out the long American drought. Jazz pianist Oscar Peterson is a Montrealer, and Canadians write weighty articles on "the Canadian jazz scene." In "pop" music, Canada has repaid America's gift of Elvis Presley with Paul Anka, an Ottawa youth equally adept at provoking hysteria in teenaged American girls.

In television, Canada fights to maintain its identity through the government-owned Canadian Broadcasting Corporation, which puts heavy emphasis on programs written by and for Canadians. Its programing—though limited by the small budget the government allows it and by the size of the potential audience for commercials (Canada has fewer than six million television sets against nearly 75 million in the U.S.)—is, nevertheless, often of a very high order. Although the CBC carries a number of

American programs, it is required by its board of governors to provide half of its programs from native sources, and many of them are excellent. However, Canadians often tune out the CBC to pick up big, expensively budgeted U.S. network shows where they come in from American stations along the border. This alarms some sociologists and politicians—particularly in Quebec, where clerical censorship and provincial policies have long insulated rural communities from the North American experience. But while French Canadian parents still tune in to the CBC's French channel, their children are learning a new way of life via American situation comedies and Westerns.

American magazines such as LIFE and *Look* are widely read in Canada as are the Canadian editions of TIME and *The Reader's Digest*. The *Digest* sells more copies than *Chatelaine,* the most popular Canadian magazine. As for Canadian newspapers, even those that once tried to resemble the staid London *Times* have now switched from an English to an American format. They carry U.S. columnists and comic strips and frequently use U.S. news agencies for coverage of foreign affairs. Their editorial policies, however, consciously reflect their own Canadian approach to national and international problems, and many of them are developing native-born columnists to replace the Art Buchwalds and Sheilah Grahams who have long been Canadians' standard reading fare.

IF, on the whole, many Canadian newspapers are not shining examples of American journalism, some Canadian newspaper owners are publishing wizards. Combining Canadian shrewdness with an awesome grasp of U.S. operating methods, they have blossomed as considerable press lords abroad. The late Lord Beaverbrook, born plain Max Aitken and raised in Newcastle, New Brunswick, was long a British public figure, ubiquitous as a London fog, largely through the success of his *Daily Express,* a combination of ultra-Tory editorials and snappy news stories which more than four million Britons read over breakfast. Roy Thomson, now Lord Thomson of Fleet and the multimillionaire owner of newspapers in seven countries, including the U.S., Scotland, Canada and England (where his holdings include the influential London *Times*), started with one small-town newspaper in Timmins, Ontario.

IN sport, Canada has both borrowed and given. Ice hockey, which Canadians developed in its modern form, is now played all over Europe, in the U.S. and in Russia. Small-town Canadian teams, often financed by their local Chambers of Commerce, used to journey to Olympic games, returning in triumph with the medal. Since 1952 the opposition has improved and Canadians, who play a rougher type of hockey than anyone else, have become the defeated heavies at several international meets. Canadian amateurs play rough in emulation of their best players, who, as highly paid professionals, are ineligible for Olympic competition. In fact, these professionals make up the entire playing force—except for an occasional lonely American or two—of the 10 American teams in the National Hockey League. Canada, of course, has two officially Canadian teams in the League, the Montreal Canadiens and the Toronto Maple Leafs.

The Americans reciprocate by providing the majority of Canada's best professional football players.

If, as sociologists and psychiatrists believe, sport is a release for hidden aggressions, then Canadians must be among the world's angriest peoples. While they are enthusiastic about baseball and while they excel in such peaceful sports as curling, figure skating and swimming, these remain minority pursuits. Professional football and professional hockey—the rougher the better—arouse more Canadians to greater enthusiasm than any other subject or cause. When two strangers meet anywhere in Canada, they discuss, not the weather, but last night's hockey scores or last season's football games. Canadian football, incidentally, started out as a fairly open game with rules limiting blocking, but the fans, becoming accustomed to

American football which they watch on television, have acquiesced in changes that have removed some of the Canadian distinctions and made their game almost as rough as American football.

But by far the most important factors in Canadian assimilation of American ways are, of course, a shared language and proximity. If Canadians sometimes complain that they are being deluged with American popular fiction, they themselves have made important contributions to its body of works. Americans have avidly consumed the novels of Ontario's Mazo de la Roche, the humorous sketches of Stephen Leacock, a McGill University professor, and the children's books of Lucy Maude Montgomery, author of *Anne of Green Gables.* Thomas Chandler Haliburton, creator of Sam Slick, the archetypical Yankee drummer, was Canadian, as was Frank L. Packard, one of the most popular adventure-story writers of the post-Victorian era. In our day, Thomas B. Costain has shown that Midas touch which leads to hundreds of thousands of American sales and extravagant film versions of his novels.

CANADIANS have used U.S. labor-saving devices as long as have Americans; they have benefited from every U.S. technological advance, have read Gesell, Spock and Freud, and have worried about conspicuous consumption, rock and roll, Madison Avenue advertising and juvenile delinquency in the same period and in much the same way as their U.S. neighbors. By now, they tend to think of these things not as foreign but as their own. And at the same time that they become more American in their tastes, they continue to cherish regional myths. Each major section of Canada sees itself as apart from all others. Each cultivates its difference, each dreams a dream which has little to do with reality.

Thus, in the Maritime provinces of Nova Scotia, New Brunswick and Prince Edward Island, the regional myth is mainly Scots. Men wear the kilt on special occasions, and some children are still taught the Gaelic tongue. Theirs is a static society, proud and poor, little touched by the successive waves of immigration that have changed the complexion of other provinces. Maritimers think of themselves as "the chosen people of Canada" and are proud that, through their universities, their major export to other provinces is brains. Bankers, university presidents and politicians across the country often turn out to be Maritimers. They have a friendly feeling towards New England, whence many of their ancestors came, but not for the rest of America. As for the other provinces of Canada, Quebec is, to Maritimers, a sinful place where young bloods go on wild weekends; Ontario is "Upper Canada" and "far too high-pressure"; the West and British Columbia are unknown countries.

QUEBEC'S regional myth is the province's glorious French past. Bolstered by a different language, the area draws heavily on the past to preserve its difference from the rest of Canada. Politicians employ such slogans as "Let us be ourselves" *(Rester d'abord nous-mêmes)* and "Our master, the past" in an effort to retain their identity and combat a growing Anglicization—or Americanization—of the province. "Be ourselves," as Canadian historians have pointed out, is close kin to the slogan of the militant Irish Republican Army—"Ourselves alone"—and is thus the opposite of what the Fathers of Confederation intended when they tried to make a Canadian nation by uniting Quebec with English Canada. Today, Quebec tries with some difficulty to combine its drive for modernization and industrialization with a heightened emphasis on its glorious, mythical and separate past.

In prosperous, busy Ontario, the regional myth is English. The capital, Toronto, has long been a national standing joke for its blue laws, Sabbath closings and air of Presbyterian righteousness. In its miasma of winding residential avenues, an English visitor will experience the shock of recognition—a vision of parks and prams, of lives of quiet desperation lived out to the clatter of teacups and the ringing of dinner gongs. Yet downtown Toronto is a city of ugly vitality whose stock exchange is the world's third largest in volume of trading and, although Toronto was long a stronghold of the pro-British, anti-Catholic, anti-French Canadian and anti-American Loyal Orange Association, it is now the area most popular with both European and U.S. immigrants.

THE older buildings and quadrangles of Toronto's university are poor provincial copies of their Oxford and Cambridge originals, but the university is Canada's best, and Toronto's magnificent Royal Ontario Museum has, among other treasures, one of the finest collections of Chinese art in the West. Ontario is one of the three Canadian provinces which are larger than Texas. A rich agricultural region, it also contains Canada's most highly developed industrial complex, with a network of 14,000 plants producing more than $17 billion worth of goods a year. It has more than one third of the nation's purchasing power, and the national capital, Ottawa, is within its boundaries, a fact which contributes to Ontario's feeling of total self-sufficiency. Well run, relatively free from corruption and, in reality, more Americanized than any other part of the country, it thinks of itself as an island of British probity surrounded on the north by arctic snows, on the west by Prairie farmers (many of Middle European extraction), on the east by French Quebec and to the south by Yankees.

The Prairie provinces of Alberta, Saskatchewan and Manitoba long cherished the myth of being Canada's "have nots," remembering the Great Depression when rich Eastern bankers were the unseen enemy. Throughout the 1930s these provinces, which were then almost entirely agricultural, endured a cycle of disaster that reads like the Book of Lamentations. They suffered drought, grasshoppers, low farm prices, unemployment, hunger and dispossession. Since World War II, however, the discovery and development of gas and oil reserves and other large mineral deposits, as well as improved farm prices, have made them as prosperous as any province in Canada. Compared with the Maritimes and Newfoundland, they are booming and they hold enormous potential for development. The regional myth of being the underdog is largely dead except in political oratory.

British Columbia, long sealed off from the rest of Canada by the Rockies, persists in the myth of the wild, untrammeled frontier, and its inhabitants, even in the jet age, think of Montreal and Toronto as cities in a far-off foreign land. The British Columbia myth has tendrils in reality, for the climate is mild, the prospect pleasing and the people are the Californians of Canada, open, self-confident and hedonistic. Canadian caution is cast aside, Confederation is ignored and British Columbians live completely on a North-South axis. They shop in Seattle; their department stores advertise in Seattle newspapers and on Seattle television stations, and if they think of a vacation trip to the big city, that city usually is San Francisco. Even Victoria, the provincial capital, long a haven for British remittance men and retired colonels, is losing its English patina. The frontier myth has been transformed into a vision of the New Frontier, and British Columbians are becoming the prototypes of the Canadian North Americans of tomorrow.

EACH of these regional myths of nationality and special temperament is fading today before the osmotic pull of American life. While Canadians have increasingly adapted American ways to their special needs, they have not yet resolved the struggle between history and geography. As André Siegfried, the Alexis de Tocqueville of Canada, said of them almost 40 years ago: "The weakness is that of a country which is hybrid and divided, and which is not sure of itself. It cannot choose between the United States and England without destroying itself in the process. Hence arises the uncertainty of a heterogeneous people . . . who are not sure they want the degree of cultural unity . . . necessary for the definite achievement of their personality."

The village choir of Drake, Saskatchewan, a tiny farm community on the Prairies, rehearses vigorously in the town church.

Subtle Shadings in the Inherited Ways of Life

Canada fell heir to two great cultures, English and French, and it continues to be influenced in everything from philosophy to fashions by the two lands that jointly gave it birth. But Canada is huge and wild in comparison with its small, long-settled parent countries. As a result, both Canada's cultural heritage and its current borrowings have undergone changes as they have been adapted to a new environment. The result is a Canadian look—not quite British in English Canada, not quite French in Quebec and, despite the pressure of proximity, not quite American anywhere. Unmistakable although largely indescribable, this subtly different look is visible in the peoples' pastimes and sports, their manners and their institutions.

BEJEWELED CROWD attends a ball held in a big Toronto department store

COOLLY ELEGANT LADIES pause between dances at the Symphony Ball near a flower-decked picture of Beethoven. The proceeds of the ball help support the city's symphony orchestra.

INFLUENTIAL TORONTONIANS in white tie and tails share a joke as their wives chat. The man on the right is Benjamin Luxenberg, a leading Toronto lawyer and a patron of the arts.

WALTZING COUPLES cast shadows on the floor *(opposite)* as they dance to music provided by members of the symphony orchestra. The store's main restaurant was cleared for the ball.

GOVERNMENT DIGNITARIES, including the former lieutenant governor of Ontario *(facing camera)* and his kilted aide, gather with women of the committee which arranges the ball.

THE PARISIAN LOOK *is strong among the young people who frequent Left*

Bank-style clubs in downtown Montreal

SPACE-AGE DISCOTHÈQUE, La Mousse Spacthèque, attracts a jostling crowd of dancers. Designed by controversial artist Jean Paul Mousseau, it has a ceiling hung with cork stalactites.

HIPPIE HANGOUT, Le Drug, is decorated with cavelike colored walls and has an electronic coordination of light and music that theoretically gives the dancers a psychedelic experience.

YOUNG SOPHISTICATES converse under a catacomb arch at the cluttered bar *(left)* of Montreal's first discothèque, La Licorne. This nightclub is designed to resemble a Parisian *cave*.

NEW VIGOR in the theater and other arts challenges the old enthusiasm for games and the heroes of sport

CONQUERING HEROES of the Toronto Maple Leafs hockey team are presented with the Stanley Cup in 1967 by Clarence Campbell *(left)*, president of the National Hockey League. The Cup was won four times by the Leafs in the mid-1960s.

REHEARSING ACTORS run through their parts in the courtyard of La Poudrière, an old powder storehouse that has been made into a theater by Montreal's International Theater company. Various groups present plays here in five languages.

OUTDOOR PLEASURES continue to delight a majority of the Canadian people

IN ICY WATERS, the river banks still covered with snow, Roderick Haig-Brown, an eloquent writer on the pleasures of angling, casts for steelheads in British Columbia's Heber River.

AMONG WINTER ICE FLOES, brightly dressed teams race their large canoes across the St. Lawrence River in Quebec harbor. This race is part of Quebec's yearly winter carnival.

SALUTING THEIR MONARCH, Canadian troops present arms as Queen Elizabeth and Prince Philip stand in the ornately Gothic archway of Ottawa's Peace Tower. During her visit to Canada, the Queen presided over Parliament's opening session.

5

Clubmen and the Other Club

THERE is no such person as Stewart Henderson McMaster, yet he is easily invented. Almost certainly his name will have a Scottish ring. He is English on his mother's side, and his wife, the granddaughter of an Anglican bishop, is also of English descent. He is a director of two or more of Canada's dominant business corporations, a university governor, an executive member of the Canadian Manufacturers' Association and the Canadian Chamber of Commerce. He sits on the board of more than a dozen charitable institutions.

McMaster is in his late fifties, plays golf and exercises on a horse which he keeps in a riding academy. Some of his suits are still double-breasted because they were made for him in London and last beautifully. He wears his hair a little longer than do Americans, but not quite so long as an Englishman. He always wears a waistcoat and favors white or conservatively striped shirts with small-patterned ties. Most days he drops in at his club, which is the most exclusive in town. He belongs to other exclusive clubs in other Canadian cities, paying a thousand dollars a year in dues. His friends call him "Stu." Abbreviations and nicknames are the rule in his business circle for he has known some of these men since his private-school days. Others he met as fellow students in the engineering and law schools of McGill or the University of Toronto. Like McMaster, they are among the 760 most powerful industrial and commercial leaders in Canada.

A 1957 study by John Porter, a Canadian sociologist, showed that of the 760 men who then made up Canada's economic elite, 611 were born in Canada, 76 in the United States, 64 in Britain and nine in other countries. The study confirms what historians have always known, namely, that the economic development of Canada has been, and is, largely in the hands of the English Canadians. This, of course, is not very different from the situation in the eastern United States, where Top People traditionally have had Anglo-Scots names and have been similarly conditioned at the right prep schools, the right Ivy League colleges, the right clubs and the right summer places. In neither country is this background a guarantee of a rigid set of opinions, and therefore our imaginary Mr. McMaster is by no means representative of all of the English Canadian corporate elite. Yet it is reasonable to suggest that his attitudes represent the majority opinion of what can be called the Canadian Establishment.

STU McMASTER does not consider himself British. He is Canadian. Of course his people came from the British Isles. They weren't "foreigners." He believes that other nationalities, except the French, are not really Canadians. Last time he was in London, he and his wife were presented to the Queen at her annual garden party. It was a great moment. The British way of life made Canada what it is today and Stu McMaster thinks no one should ever forget that point. But he is critical of British business methods. Englishmen simply don't understand Canada and lack the get-up-and-go to sell in the Canadian market. The Americans, on the other hand, take far too many financial risks.

He is not anti-American, mind you. Far from it. Some of his friends went to college in the States and he knows a number of Americans in his business. Still, they are not quite his dish. Always pouring money into research and complaining about delivery dates and costs that run over estimates. They simply don't understand the way things are done up here.

French Canadians? Yes, he knows one or two, good fellows who speak English perfectly. Nowadays, some firms think it politic to have one French Canadian on their board of directors. McMaster doesn't agree. Like many English Canadians he believes that most French Canadians are poorly educated and unsuited for responsible posts. He believes this without ever having put his prejudice to the test. There were (according to Porter's study) only 51 French Canadians among the 760 members of the corporate elite. They got there through French Canadian law firms, important political affiliations or directorships in French Canadian banks.

McMASTER is an Anglican. Many of his business friends are Presbyterians or members of the United Church of Canada. Very few are Roman Catholics. Although Canada was 43 per cent Catholic according to Porter's survey, there were then only 78 Catholics (about 10 per cent) in the corporate elite, most of them, of course, French Canadians. There were only six Jews in the corporate elite, and all were either in the liquor industry or in one of the smaller corporations. Jews are not members of Stu McMaster's clubs. Stu McMaster was not born poor. His forebears had a stake in Canada's business. After training as an engineer, Stu entered the family firm, but this pattern of entering the family business does not extend to all of his friends. However, most of them had business connections and trained for their careers accordingly. There are very few old-style entrepreneurs in the elite, and the majority have made their careers within the large corporate system. Engineers, like Stu McMaster, and scientists make up the largest group in the corporate hierarchy, although, at the top, their duties are likely to be purely administrative. Lawyers are the second largest group. After them come bankers and brokers. Banking, in the old Scottish tradition, is the one way left for a poor boy to reach the corporate heights. Of the 23 top Canadian bankers, only one went to a university. The rest took an average of 38 years to crawl from teller's cage to board room.

The newspapers like to cite these bankers as evidence that Canada is a land of unlimited opportunity. But Stewart Henderson McMaster, sitting in the Mount Royal Club in Montreal, or the York in Toronto, will allow himself a small smile. Those bankers are old men. Today, without the right private school, the right college and the right clubs, even a Scotsman has a hard time of it. To be sure, this system limits the competition. Outside of Quebec (which has a different form of schooling), only about five per cent of Canadian boys go to private schools.

Stu McMaster lives in the best suburb of his city in a comfortable house with a garden. The house is not ostentatious. In fact, many of the men who work for him live in similar houses. Canadians, outside of Montreal and Toronto, are not apartment dwellers, and quite far down on the social scale a separate or semidetached house is the norm. However, although prudently unostentatious at home, McMaster has a ski lodge up north and, while he does not show off about this either, he owns a very expensive "cottage" in an exclusive resort colony in Nassau. He and the family like to get down there for a week or so to break the long winter.

HIS wife dresses simply in a rather English style: cashmere sweaters, pearl necklace, tweeds. And, of course, a good mink coat. She buys most of her clothes from the better Canadian department stores, which have branches in every major city and offer the same styles in each. Thus, like many other Canadian women, Mrs. McMaster tends to seem somewhat standardized in her dress. Scaasi, a Montreal-born designer who now makes expensive clothes worn by Americans, complains that Canadian women lack chic and "dress according to their age."

As for the McMaster children, the eldest boy, after training as an engineer, entered the family business. The second, who trained as a scientist, found a promising position with a large petrochemicals firm, of which Stu is a director. The McMaster girl "came out" as a debutante a few years ago and married a boy she dated during her deb year. Both sons and daughter ski, dance, dine and attend parties within a very small group, most of whom they have known since childhood. Like members of most such intimate groups, they feel uncomfortable with outsiders.

AT election time McMaster votes Conservative, although a large proportion of the corporate elite votes Liberal. He doesn't think there's much difference nowadays. The Liberals were in power for a long time and business didn't suffer. It was the Liberals, however, who inaugurated a government-subsidized hospital insurance plan which, in some of the provinces, takes care of most hospital charges, drug expenses and doctors' fees for qualified persons. Stu McMaster believes this is the thin edge of the wedge for a complete socialized medicine scheme, much like the one in Britain. He disapproves. He also disapproves of the old-age security act, which entitles everybody, even the prime minister, to $75 a month at age 65.

He strongly opposes the family allowance scheme whereby each Canadian child under 10 years of age receives six dollars a month. For children between 10 and 16 years of age, eight dollars a month is paid. In McMaster's opinion this is just an invitation to the French Canadians to go ahead with what their politicians have long called "the revenge of the cradle." The Dionne quintuplets were French Canadian, after all. And in rural Quebec, he has been told, 15 in a family is not unusual. He has been told that French Canadian nationalists are still boasting that, in the not too distant future, their people will outnumber his. He agrees. But his fears are exaggerated. Quebec's birth rate is only slightly greater than that of the more populous English-speaking province of Ontario, and the highest birth rate in any Canadian province is in English-speaking Newfoundland.

The new government medical insurance plan has, of course, helped Toronto's hospitals and lightened somewhat McMaster's committee work. For he, in common with other members of the economic elite, used to spend a great deal of time raising money for hospitals. He still devotes himself to a number of such philanthropic activities. If a man is making his way up in the corporate hierarchy he will be asked to chair a Special Names committee. Top men are asked to chair a campaign and are expected to exceed the campaign objective. It is one way their abilities can be judged by other leaders of the business community. As McMaster says, even philanthropy has a way of showing up on your balance sheet.

McMaster gives some money to the symphony orchestra and the art gallery in his city because it is expected of him. He finds it quite astonishing that people like the Rockefellers really seem to *like* art. Most Canadian multimillionaires prefer to endow universities and hospitals, and the rest of the corporate elite follow suit. As for reading, a cynical old corporation lawyer recently remarked in Montreal: "The only books the rich read in Canada are bankbooks."

Yet these same men, many of whom got a very specialized education and understand few subjects other than engineering, corporation law and finance, have enormous control over the policies of Canada's major universities. Academic cynics have grumblingly suggested that some of these industrial leaders are less than passionately exercised over the question of improving university educational standards but continue to seek university governorships because they represent *the* top status symbol in the corporate world.

ODDLY enough, despite this closed clubmen's world of honors and special privileges, "rags to riches to rags in four generations" is still a fairly common occurrence in Canada. Few of the very rich families seem to have developed a lasting continuity of achievement. And while the corporate and social elites of English Canada still maintain a strong pro-British bias, there is evidence that some of the country's top businessmen, both within and without the corporate elite group, are growing tired of their cautious, complacent, snobbish colleagues. "They've got to get off their duffs," says E. P. Taylor, a multi-millionaire wheeler and dealer who is Canada's most influential business leader. As for the new nationalism, which many of the rich applaud, Taylor dismisses it with the remark, "Have you ever heard of anything more outdated?" In a corporate structure which contains both E. P. Taylor and men like Stu McMaster, there seems little doubt that the former will prevail.

THE comments of an E. P. Taylor on the nationalist new wave are anathema to another influential Canadian group. Let us call them the Other Club, for few of them have the money or the inclination to join the clubs which Stu McMaster frequents. Members of the Other Club include civil servants, university professors, diplomats, writers and newspaper pundits. They are men with a cause and that cause is the survival of Canada as an independent nation within the British Commonwealth, wholly free from American influence. They are seekers after national greatness and believe, in a very British way, that other nations will be influenced by Canada's example. The Other Club is growing. It has discovered in anti-Americanism a rallying cry that has at last gained it a wide national following. And behind its stance of "my country right or wrong," it incurs the charge that its members are themselves the new Canadian Establishment, busily engaged in putting up barriers against any outside influence which threatens to rob them of their authority.

Our imaginary member of the Other Club has, like Stu McMaster, an Anglo-Scots name. Let us call him Gordon Bruce Howard. His father was a Presbyterian minister and he is a child of the manse. He took an honors history degree at the University of Toronto and shortly afterwards sailed for England and Oxford as one of Canada's Rhodes scholars. Together with the brightest young minds from all over the British Commonwealth, he sat in the rooms of erudite dons, sipped sherry with young revolutionaries who would become future Asian and African prime ministers, bought his first tattersall shirt and brown suede shoes, rowed for his university in the Oxford-Cambridge boat race and fell deeply, permanently and hopelessly in love with the British way of doing things. So much in love that, on his return to Canada four years later, he stood in a customs shed in Halifax, appalled by the dullness, provinciality and vulgarity of his native land. How different it was from Oxford! How American it now seemed! Someone, he decided, must change all this. Someone must make Canada a country he could be proud of.

For a few months he thought of government as a career. There were rumors of an opening in the Department of External Affairs. But then his old Oxford tutor wrote a letter to Carleton University in Ottawa, and he was promptly hired as an assistant professor of history. The capital had a small-town atmosphere reminiscent of Oxford. There were serious, stimulating gatherings of bright, British-trained young men who were doing interesting things in External Affairs, at UNESCO, or reporting back to the capital from United Nations meetings in New York. In Ottawa, in the postwar decades, the Other Club was born.

CANADA'S FOUR ATLANTIC PROVINCES

The Atlantic provinces of Canada's East Coast consist of Nova Scotia, New Brunswick and Prince Edward Island—together known as the Maritime provinces—plus the former British colony of Newfoundland, which joined Canada in 1949. Intensely loyal to Britain, the Atlantic provinces are populated by a higher proportion of British stock than any other part of Canada. Their economies are largely dependent on forestry, fishing, and the depressed coal and steel industries.

NOVA SCOTIA (New Scotland) is, as its name implies, heavily Scots in atmosphere. Many of the people are descended from the 50,000 Scots immigrants who arrived in the early 19th Century, and the province boasts the only Gaelic college in North America. Nova Scotia's capital, Halifax, is the chief city in the Maritimes and Canada's leading port and rail terminus on the Atlantic Ocean.

NEW BRUNSWICK, like most of the other Maritimes, has been depressed economically in modern times, but it has shown signs of new vigor and growth in the past decade. Its chief city, Saint John, was a thriving metropolis in the days of sail, claiming to be the world's fourth-busiest port.

PRINCE EDWARD ISLAND is Canada's smallest, most densely populated and least prosperous province. It is heavily dependent on the vagaries of the weather for its crop of excellent seed potatoes and feed grains as well as for the success of its brief summer-tourist season.

NEWFOUNDLAND was persuaded to join with Canada largely through the efforts of Premier Joseph Smallwood, who is working hard to modernize the province's economy. Predominantly of English and Irish stock, the Newfoundlanders are traditionally cod fishermen, though fishing has now ceded first place in the island's economy to the growing pulp and paper industry.

At first, Gordon Howard and his friends saw Canada as a "golden hinge" between Britain and the United States. Canadians could act as mediators and interpreters between the two great English-speaking powers. After all, Prime Minister Mackenzie King had done just that in the wartime exchanges between Roosevelt and Churchill. But in the postwar era summit conferences became the vogue, and when the heavyweight champions climbed into the ring, the seconds were usually ordered out.

Disappointed but not discouraged, Gordon Howard and his friends conceived the idea of Canada as a leader of the newly emergent and uncommitted nations. At first they did brilliantly in the United Nations, but soon, at the small dinner parties which Gordon and his friends gave for every Asian, African or other neutralist who turned up in Ottawa, they began to hear complaints against their country. Two of the complaints most often heard were that Canada was a white Commonwealth nation under Britain's heel—and with an unenlightened record itself as far as admission of colored or Asiatic immigrants was concerned—and that Canada was simply an American satellite which fell in line behind John Foster Dulles.

The members of the Other Club were dismayed. Canada's government now steered its own course in international affairs, they insisted. Look at Canada's record during the Suez crisis. Nor was Canada really like America. Far from it. Canadians would never elect a military man as head of state. Canadians would never stand for a Senator McCarthy. But the Asians, the Africans and the other neutralists merely shook their heads. Canada had fought alongside America in Korea, had it not? And what was the country's voting record at the Commonwealth conferences? That of a white dominion, was it not? As the 1960s approached, the men in Congress party caps and tarbooshes melted away. Gordon Howard and his friends reluctantly decided that Canada must find a new role.

MOST of the Other Club has traditionally voted Liberal. A few have voted for the New Democratic (socialist) party. But in 1957 Conservative leader John Diefenbaker called for a reduction of American influence in Canada's economy and closer ties with Britain. This, the Other Club decided, was their point of view, exactly. They urged new legislation to curb American investment. They spoke out for the protection of Canadian magazines and television shows. They discovered that their students were talking about some American writer called J. D. Salinger, whom Gordon Howard, deep in C. P. Snow's novelistic explorations of British university life, had never even heard of.

Members of the Other Club went on television panels to denounce the pernicious influence of Jack Paar, Ed Sullivan and *What's My Line?* Canadian audiences must be protected from this sort of thing, they said. As they did not watch television themselves, they did not know that the Canadian shows most imperiled by Jack Paar etc. were Canadian imitations of Jack Paar etc.

To their surprise the Other Club found out anti-Americanism was almost as popular with Canadians as was Americanism. For the first time in their lives, Gordon Howard and his friends gave their views, not in obscure weeklies and learned quarterlies, but in daily newspapers, in national magazines and on nationwide television shows. Some of their views became more and more radical. Canada should refuse to allow Americans to build defense installations in the Canadian North. Why, asked Gordon Howard, should Russian missiles loaded with nuclear death be knocked down by American interceptors over Canadian cities? Some Other Clubmen went even further. They advocated that Canada should pull out of NATO, renounce U.S. nuclear warheads, disarm completely and devote the money formerly spent on defense to an all-out effort to help backward nations. By becoming a nation of peace corpsmen, Canada, they felt, might influence other nations toward disarmament and good works.

Canadians, like people everywhere, wanted peace. Faced by the terrors of nuclear war, they had good reason to seek surcease in schemes for disarmament and disengagement. But, like the Scots of long ago, their country lay on the northern border of a rich and armed nation whose wishes they were forced to heed. In addition, their fears for Canada's uncertain national identity and its gradually waning influence in world affairs forced them to a position on the sidelines of issues until, as one disillusioned intellectual put it, Canada's foreign policy now "consists chiefly in preaching sermons against sin."

IN their concern for a genuinely independent Canada and in their fears for their national survival, sincere and honest men like Gordon Howard were afraid to upset the internal balance of power. By their silence they gave tacit approval to the domination of the country's majority population of French Canadians and immigrants from other European countries by the restrictive English Canadian elite. The economic and cultural alternatives they offered to American influence were, in the main, secondhand borrowings from Britain. Thus men like Gordon Howard unwittingly became partners in the complacent and snobbish Establishment founded and maintained by men like Stewart McMaster. Under their joint aegis, postwar Canada was starved of the self-criticism and self-insight necessary for its growth as an independent nation.

Cricketers from Ontario's Trinity College School, an institution modeled on Britain's public schools, take a traditional tea break.

English Formality Preserved in the New World

Despite the fact that Canada has been virtually independent of Britain for several decades, a pro-British strain still lingers in the hearts and habits of many Canadians. This is especially true in Ontario and its capital, Toronto, strongholds of the Anglo-Scots corporate elite who largely own and operate Canadian big business. Though Toronto resembles an American industrial city more than it does London, its businessmen's clubs might well be located on Pall Mall, and nearby boys' schools might be in the Oxfordshire countryside. If the ways of ancient and tiny Britain seem anachronistic in modern, mammoth Canada, that only lends them added charm in the eyes of people still struggling to achieve a settled pattern of life.

HIGH-ROOFED HALL with carved oak beams, modeled on the refectories of Oxford and Cambridge, serves as the dining room for neatly dressed senior students at Trinity College School.

ENGROSSED STUDENT at Trinity labors over a biology project on fish. Considerable individual attention is given to each student, and he is encouraged to do independent work.

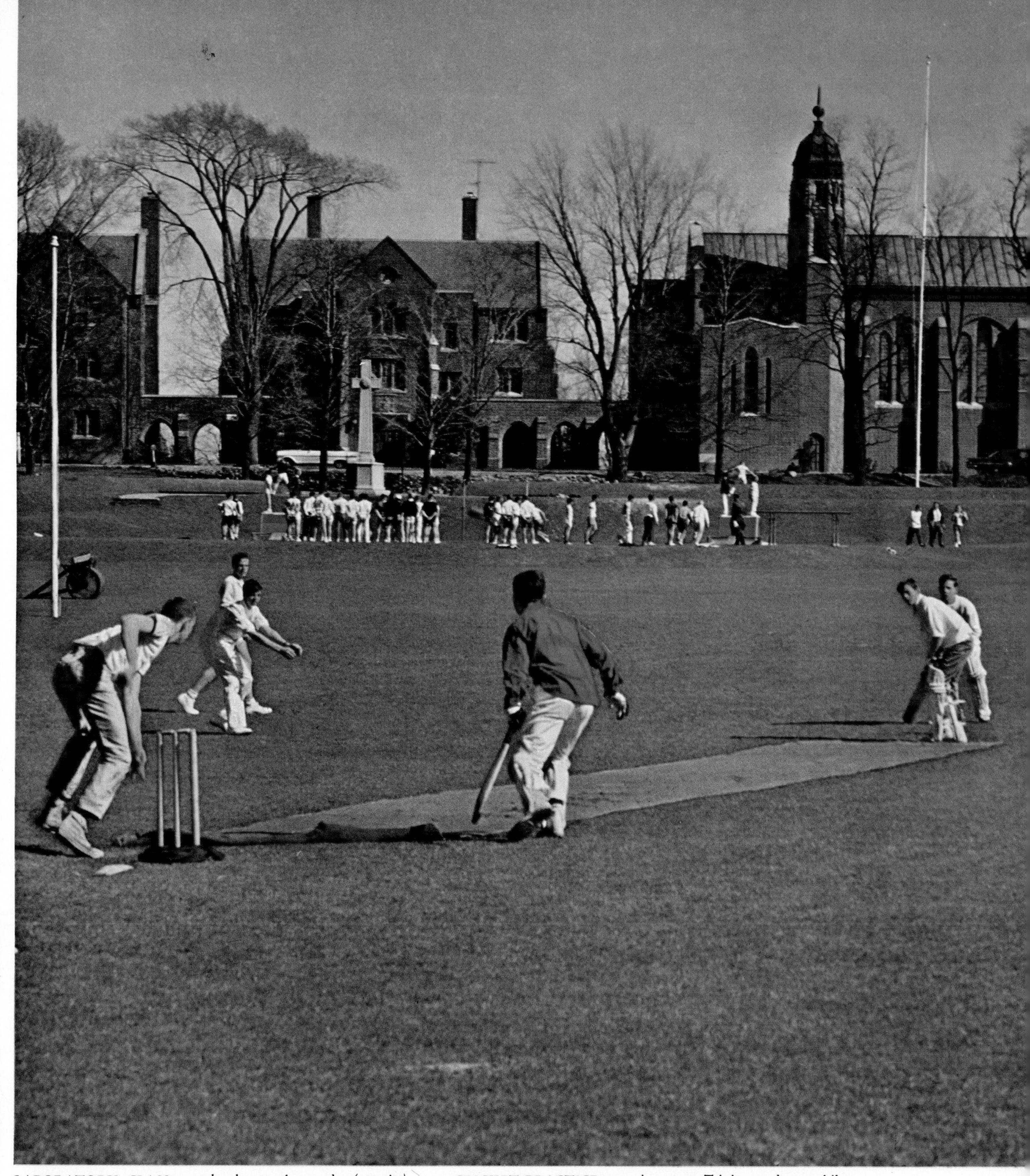

LABORATORY CLASS, notebooks at the ready *(opposite)*, encircles a chemistry instructor *(left, with glasses)*. The school's enrollment is limited, its classes small—and its tuition high.

CRICKET PRACTICE occupies some Trinity students while others engage in gymnastics *(background)*. The school's campus is in Port Hope, Ontario, 60 miles northeast of Toronto.

AN ELEGANT HORSE SHOW is a high point of the social year in Toronto

RED-JACKETED MOUNTIES put their sleek horses over jumps during Toronto's Royal Agricultural Winter Fair, which is considered the most elegant horse show in North America.

FORMALLY DRESSED CROWD watches as Brigadier F. C. Wallace *(opposite, left)*, an official of the 1959 "Royal," welcomes J. Keiller Mackay, then lieutenant governor of Ontario.

30

ROLLING FIELDS stretching toward the Quebec town of Bagotville and the Saguenay River frame a team of horses pulling a weathered farm cart. The fields and farms in this section are typical of the rural areas that have long dominated Quebec.

6

Winds of Change in Quebec

THE French of Quebec have always seemed backward and potentially dangerous to those outsiders who have ruled them. In 1730 a French official named Gilles Hocquart concluded that "they are naturally perverse." And in 1839 the brilliant Lord Durham, in a historic report on Canada, advised the British government that a French-speaking Quebec would always remain the stumbling block to effective self-government of the country. "There can hardly be conceived," he wrote, "a nationality more destitute of all that can invigorate and elevate a people, than that which is exhibited by the descendants of the French in Lower Canada, owing to their retaining their peculiar language and manners. They are a people with no history and no literature."

Despite the peculiarly English arrogance of Durham's phrases, his report accurately forecast the stumbling block posed for Canada by that country within a country which is Quebec. And although his name is still hated in French Canada because his famous report advocated the Anglicization of Quebec, his words are echoed today by French Canadians themselves. In 1960 an anonymous priest, styling himself Frère Untel, wrote a book which became Quebec's bestseller. In it he complains: "Our spirit was broken two centuries ago and it shows. . . . We are among the very few peoples who have not known a political revolution or a major religious crisis." French Canadian education, he pointed out, had no goal to achieve, "only the precipice of Protestantization and Anglicization to avoid." And when, in 1962, the Social Credit party supporters of Réal Caouette, a Quebec admirer of Hitler and Mussolini, gave him control of 26 seats in the Canadian House of Commons, Gérard Filion, the former editor and publisher of Montreal's *Le Devoir,* wrote bitterly: "Quebec is not a province like the others. She is a little more stupid."

TRUE, in the past Quebec has been no model for students of honest government. Twice as big as Texas and with one third of Canada's population, the province until 1960 had been ruled by provincial governments more concerned with building party war chests than with governing well. In 1961 a royal commission investigating the old *Union Nationale* government, which had held power for almost 16 years, estimated that the total shakedown of companies doing business with the provincial government during that period ran as high as $100 million paid in the form of "salesmen's commissions" to party politicians. A Mr. Gérald Martineau, the party treasurer, testified that he had arranged over the years for the collection and distribution to the party faithful of these business kickbacks but insisted that "I continued a system that was in force since 1935 and perhaps before." In addition, the party in power sold liquor licenses for fees which, in Montreal, ran as high as $30,000. Provincial liquor police had the right to enter and search any premises without a warrant.

Roads and schools were built in districts that voted for the provincial government but not in those districts that voted for opposition parties. Ballot boxes were stolen by election strong-arm squads and stuffed with government ballots. The provincial minister of labor, Antonio Barrette, was known openly as the "anti-labor minister" and his policies prevailed. In 1949 he used provincial police to beat up Catholic workers in a bitter four-and-a-half-month strike of miners against the Johns-Manville Company in Asbestos, Quebec.

In federal matters the province was traditionally isolationist and jealous of its provincial rights. These rights were zealously upheld by Quebec members of the federal Parliament in Ottawa, whatever their political affiliations. Quebec is allotted 75 of the 265 seats in the federal House of Commons, and until a few years ago the province's politicians and people fiercely resented any criticism of their economic backwardness or their political morals.

That such criticisms are now being voiced, not by the hated English Canadians but by French Canadians themselves, constitutes nothing less than a revolution in French Canada. For Quebec since 1960 has undergone an astonishing transformation. New forces and new movements have jostled the old politicians from their seats of power and the province is being governed by a more progressive administration that has attacked the old practices of political nepotism, graft and intimidation of opponents. Since 1960 the province has also benefited from a new and more enlightened church leadership, which has actually supported government moves to raise the province's educational standards, even though these moves sometimes conflict directly with the clergy's old hold on the Quebec school system.

AS this mood of change has gained strength, French Canadians have begun to reassess Quebec's relation to Canada's other, predominantly English-speaking provinces. Politicians have raised the ancient plaint that French Canada is being cheated of its fair share of the Canadian economic pie and that Quebec's industries and resources are under "foreign" domination. This, to French Canadians, means any ownership not French Canadian; and as the rest of Canada worries about American domination, so does Quebec worry about English Canadian control of Quebec's factories, hydroelectric power and mineral resources.

This feeling that the province is a "lone star state" somehow outside Confederation and with a different set of ideals dates back to Confederation itself in 1867, when Quebec reluctantly agreed to join the union only if its rights to its own language and code of civil law were guaranteed. When the other provinces agreed to this, the pattern of separateness was continued. It has continued to plague both Quebec and English Canada ever since.

TODAY that feeling is stronger than ever. Jacques Guay, a young French Canadian intellectual, spoke for his generation in a 1961 article that might have been written by one of his forebears. "My homeland," he said, "is, above all, Quebec. I believe in a federalism based on the existence of two nations, which recognizes Quebec as the absolute authority in all that concerns the French Canadian nation."

If the belief that Quebec is a separate "state" rather than a province of the country called Canada has not really succeeded in making Quebec into a separate nation, it has nevertheless enabled French Canadians to refute Lord Durham's ancient charge in one respect. They now have a history, if only a history of unyielding resistance to change. By their fanatic determination to look to "Our Master, the Past" (once one of their favorite election slogans) instead of to any partly Anglo-Saxon present, they have succeeded in preserving Quebec as the least American region in North America. By retaining their "peculiar language and manners," they have made their province a delight for the visitor, if not for their own people; a strangely European America, poignant and vivid as a small wild rose growing amid the uniform blooms of a nursery garden.

In the villages of Quebec, the houses have high, gracefully sloping roofs that do not trap the snow, walls three feet thick to keep out chills, low doorways and small windows; they face flush on the street. Passing them, the visitor is reminded of villages in Brittany or Holland. The church will be the largest building by far, usually of gray stone with a gleaming silvery roof and a large statue of the Virgin in its ample surrounding grounds. Wayside shrines abound. The curé, in long black soutane, leads a procession of little boys, knickerbockered and sashed in their First Communion suits. In winter the snow is crisp underfoot and there is a clean smell of burning wood from the ancient Quebec stoves in the village kitchens. The language is an old-fashioned peasant French, slurred and imprecise, corrupted by many odd words such as "le char" for "l'auto" and "la job" instead of "le travail"—words which are sometimes American slang transformed by accent into a new and hybrid tongue.

Even in Montreal, Canada's largest city, with its Hilton hotels, split-level suburbs and multi-lane expressways, the impact of America is constantly challenged by that combination of clerical austerity and peasant joviality which was the old style of Quebec. The old style may still be glimpsed in city squares adorned with neglected statues, in the duplex apartments whose upper floors are reached by winding iron outdoor staircases, in the gray outlines of clerical buildings which, surrounded by large, formal grounds, squat like fortresses amid the most crowded and valuable sections of the city. It can be seen also in the gaunt seminarian faces of young French Canadians—faces oddly wrong for their bright-hued city clothes.

ITS English, or contrary, posture is reflected in the haughty, determined step of an old English Canadian merchant in Montreal marching down Beaver Hall Hill towards St. James Street, wearing a long raccoon coat, a black Persian lamb hat rammed tight over his ears. St. James Street is the Wall Street of Canada and the old merchant does business with settlements all the way to the Pacific. He lives in an English district of Montreal which has its own English-appointed city administrator, police force and garbage system. He does not speak French. He is alarmed and frightened by the new French Canada's hopes and dreams. For his purposes the old French Canada was best. He welcomed the clerical dream of an agricultural society, isolated by religion, language and custom from the Canadian mainstream. He and his kind were a part of that mainstream. If French Canadians had opted out of it, so much the better for him. It left Montreal's English merchants as masters of Quebec's industrial might.

Nowadays, even the priests no longer believe in the dream of Quebec as an agricultural society going its separate way. Less than one tenth of Quebec's population still lives on farms, and in the cities and larger towns a growing absenteeism from church attendance has caused the clergy to review its policies in an effort to regain its voice as the keeper of Quebec's moral conscience. Liberal clerical forces, led by the metropolitan clergy and often acting in opposition to the more conservative rural bishops, have been leading supporters of the new government in its attempt to give the people of Quebec an improved scientific and engineering training and to modernize, and raise the general level of, the province's schools.

This wind of change was born on September 7, 1959, when Premier Maurice Duplessis, who had ruled Quebec for more than 18 years as boss of the *Union Nationale* party and virtual dictator of Quebec politics, suffered a stroke and died. At the time, however, few people were aware that a change was coming. The party had an heir apparent ready in the person of the Honorable Paul Sauvé, a Duplessis lieutenant who was known to be more liberal in his outlook than the old chief. Sauvé instituted some reforms, but, unfortunately for the machine, he died less than four months after Duplessis. The party then chose Antonio Barrette, the minister of labor who had become so well known for his antilabor efforts. It was a fatal choice.

The traditional opposition forces rallied under the banner of the Liberal party, long a power in Quebec politics. The new provincial leader chosen by the Liberals was Jean Lesage, 51, a polished politician who had been tested in government on a larger scale as minister for northern affairs in the federal government. Lesage was in the Liberal party tradition of Sir Wilfrid Laurier and Louis St. Laurent, the two French Canadians who had become prime ministers of Canada. He came to Quebec already wearing the mantle of success in national politics.

In June 1960, Lesage and the Liberal party swept to victory at the Quebec polls. The once all-powerful *Union Nationale* was badly defeated. To Quebec's voters a Liberal victory was, in itself, no guarantee of immunity from political corruption, for in the 1920s and 1930s, when Liberal governments ran Quebec, graft had been part of the political pattern.

But this new government was different. Lesage correctly sensed that urban middle-class voters wanted much more widespread reforms than Sauvé or Barrette had envisaged. This was particularly true in Montreal, which, with its 2.4 million people, contains close to half of Quebec's population. In addition, the new government was supported by influential labor leaders, journalists, and a large group of university professors and civil servants who had long rankled under the English Canadian assumption that the people of Quebec were backward and inefficient. When the more farseeing clerics joined forces with this new group, many rural districts switched to follow.

Reformers in Quebec's new government promptly advocated that the government take over control of the province's immense hydroelectric power plants, which were largely in the hands of a group of English Canadian firms.

QUEBEC'S SYMBOLIC FLAG

The white and azure flag of Quebec reminds French Canadians of their history and heritage. It

closely resembles in design the family standard of the Sieur de Maisonneuve, founder of Montreal. It also resembles the flag Jacques Cartier planted on New France and the ensigns used by French merchant ships of Champlain's era. The white cross symbolizes the Christian faith, and the fleur-de-lis, of course, is a symbol of the French monarchy.

This move shocked the province into a realization that the Liberal party might possibly intend to carry out its election pledges, a thing hitherto unheard of in Quebec. The government reformed the old liquor police and began issuing liquor licenses to restaurants for the nominal fee of $100. Word got around that companies doing business in the province need no longer start out by making a visit to the party treasurer in Quebec City. The citadels of graft and corruption had fallen, and in 1962 a delighted electorate voted the new provincial government back into power with an even greater majority than before.

BUT the idyll could not last. The inevitable backlash came from Quebec's rural areas, where traditionally conservative farmers began to grow restive under the Liberal reforms. The main cause for resentment was economic, for many of the Liberal programs had hit the farmers where it hurt most—in their pocketbooks. By abolishing patronage, the government had deprived farmers of badly needed contracts. Worse yet, the cost of road building, hydroelectric projects and educational reforms had resulted in a phenomenal rise in taxes, which in some areas soared as high as 400 per cent. Rural discontent grew so strong that in 1965 an army of some 10,000 irate farmers marched on the provincial capital at Quebec City chanting, "*La belle province,* how charming! Come see the peasants starving."

The denouement came with the elections of 1966, when a resuscitated *Union Nationale* won control once again of the provincial government. The man most responsible for the victory was Daniel Johnson, a former lieutenant of Maurice Duplessis who had become the leader of the *Union Nationale* forces during their six years as an opposition party, and who was now Quebec's new premier. Like Duplessis, Johnson won his major following from Quebec's conservatives. He stomped through the countryside to glean support at the grass-roots level, promising an elaborate program of aid to farmers and listening sympathetically to the complaints of old-guard clergymen, who felt that Liberal educational reforms were depriving them of control over the Quebec school system.

But unlike Duplessis, who had run his administration like a circus ringmaster, the new premier was no demagogue. While Duplessis had shown an almost paranoiac intolerance for critics—he cut off opposition speakers in the provincial legislature with rude cries of "Sit down, you!"—Johnson actually courted the opinions of his political adversaries. In attempting to revitalize the *Union Nationale,* Johnson sought out bright young candidates, and consulted—to their astonishment—Quebec's generally liberal intellectuals. With this timely transfusion of new blood and fresh viewpoints, Johnson seemed to have cured the party of its old ills of graft and corruption. Rather than reversing the momentum of reform begun under the Liberal party, he merely tried to alter its direction, channeling some of its benefits into the parched rural areas.

ONE fundamental plank in the *Union Nationale* party platform remained unchanged from the old days, however. The Duplessis war cry had always been that Quebec was in danger of being Anglicized and deprived of its identity. This claim reawakened deep fears and resentments among French Canadians that date back to the defeat of Montcalm by Britain's General Wolfe on the Plains of Abraham in Quebec City in 1759, and that still constitute the most powerful force in Quebec's politics. Johnson in 1965 had come out with a straightforward demand for "equality or independence" for Quebec, warning that if the province were not guaranteed a special status, giving it in effect equality with the combined provinces of English Canada, it would cease to be a part of the Canadian federation.

Such appeals to Quebec nationalism cut across party lines and struck a responsive chord with urban progressives as well as rural conservatives. Many of the supporters of the defeated Liberal party had been students and intellectuals in search of a champion for French Canadian rights, and they had hoped that the Liberal reforms would free Quebec's industries and natural resources from English Canadian control and would help to secure for French Canadians better posts in the federal government. "We've been Canada's white Negroes long enough," claimed an angry young poet. "We want our share."

French Canadians are justifiably angry at English Canadian domination of federal institutions. While the French make up almost one third of Canada's population, they hold only about 13 per cent of responsible federal jobs. In the armed forces, until very recently, the high command was almost 100 per cent English-speaking. Discrimination against French Canadians on the top levels of big corporations only recently began to be somewhat ameliorated. Montreal-born Marcel Vincent became the first French Canadian president of the Bell Telephone Company of Canada in 1963. All 17 of the company's top officers at the time were English Canadian.

In 1962, the Canadian National Railway president, Donald Gordon, was the object of violent French Canadian wrath when a number of newspapers interpreted some remarks he had made to a parliamentary committee to mean that he believed French Canadians lacked the necessary education to become railroad vice presidents. Students burned his effigy in Montreal's Place Ville Marie, and the situation was worsened when N. R. Crump, president of the Canadian Pacific Railway, announced that his railroad didn't have any French Canadian vice presidents either. Crump's excuse was that Quebec's "classical education doesn't tend to fit into our type of situation."

THAT this remark was less a rational objection than a restatement of old English Canadian prejudices became quite evident when a Toronto newspaperman turned up the facts. Of the 30 English Canadian vice presidents of the two railroads, only seven had received training which would specially qualify them for high posts in railroad management. Gordon himself had never gone to college, and Crump had taken his engineering degree long after he started working for the railroad.

This showing up of English prejudice delights the Separatists, a highly vocal splinter group which advocates that Quebec break out of Confederation altogether and become an independent state. They are militantly hostile to English Canada, the federal government and English domination of French Canada's industries. Occasionally, this animosity has erupted into violence, as in the spring of 1963, when a group of terrorists in Montreal planted homemade bombs in mail collection boxes and around federal buildings. The resulting explosions killed one person and maimed another.

THE Separatist movement continued to gain momentum, and by 1967 it had become a major factor in Quebec politics. The key figure in the movement was René Lévesque, a former television commentator who had served in the defeated Liberal administration, first as Minister of Natural Resources and then as Minister of Social Welfare. Under Lévesque's leadership, separatism gained both popularity and political respectability. As the field general and intellectual champion of many of the Liberal reforms, Lévesque had become the instant hero of Quebec's younger generation of intelligentsia, including an important number of the province's teachers, editors, writers and communications leaders. With this impressive following, Lévesque quit the Liberal Party in 1967 to found the *Souveraineté-Association,* dedicated to turning Quebec into an independent nation. "We can't be an inner colony any longer," he said. "You know, quaint old Quebec—a sort of nice reservation inside the country." The alternative to separatism, he claimed, would be the complete and irrevocable loss of French Canada's language, culture and unique personality.

But there were weaknesses in the Separatist doctrine, and the dangers in Quebec's trying to go it alone were underlined by Paul Sauriol, a writer for *Le Devoir:* "It is our economic servitude which makes possible the political and financial domination of English Canada over Quebec. And in this lies the key obstacle to practicable political Separatism. The economic reprisals on our shaky economy would leave us most vulnerable. But if our economic dependence makes Separatism impossible, the converse is also true. . . . If we had a measure of economic independence, Separatism would become less desirable."

Aside from economic considerations, other factors worked against the pull of Separatist forces. The federal government in Ottawa had begun a concentrated effort to hold Quebec within the Confederation. As early as 1963, it had set up the Royal Commission on Bilingualism and Biculturalism to investigate French Canadian grievances. The first volume of the Commission's report, whose preparation had cost $7.5 million, was issued in 1967; it emphasized the magnitude of the problem with a warning that Canada was "passing through the greatest crisis in its history." Its recommendations included sweeping language reforms as a partial solution. The report stated that both English and French should be given equal status by law in the national Parliament, the federal courts, government and administration. It also advised that all provinces and local districts with large French populations should provide schooling, government and judicial services in both English and French.

POSSIBLY even more important than its specific proposals, the Bilingualism and Biculturalism report focused the attention of the entire nation on the problem of Quebec. Its recommendations implied a readiness on the part of English Canadians to make concessions to the French in a concerted effort to repair relations, and to keep Quebec within the federation. With the more moderate elements in the province, the effort seemed to be a success. Premier Johnson, in part reacting against extremists such as Lévesque, but also taking advantage of Ottawa's apparent willingness to listen to his views, if not to buy them wholesale, modified his slogan of "equality or independence" by emphasizing the first alternative at the expense of the second one. Though "equality" to Johnson meant a special status for Quebec, he still maintained: "I am a Canadian and I want to remain a Canadian." Since he was above all a political pragmatist, acutely sensitive to the feelings of his constituency, he probably spoke for a majority of Quebec's French Canadians.

THE issue of Quebec nationalism caught the attention of the world in the summer of 1967, during a visit by Charles de Gaulle. The French president had flown to Montreal to view Expo 67, the extravagantly successful world's fair that had been built to commemorate the 100th anniversary of the Canadian Confederation. In a speech at Montreal's city hall, De Gaulle astonished everyone by shouting "Long Live Free Quebec," a Separatist battle cry. There was instant consternation not only in Ottawa but in most other capitals around the world, and the chaos was later compounded when Paris started dealing with Quebec as if it were already a separate state.

But even more than De Gaulle's statement, Expo itself had focused the world's eyes on French Canada. The fair's extraordinary success—some 50 million visitors had shown up to gawk at its dramatic exhibits—had made it the major international exposition of the century. Since most of the design, administration and execution of the fair had been in the hands of French Canadians, who held five of the nine top jobs, this triumph had meant a tremendous boost to French Canadian self-esteem. Despite the interference of De Gaulle, it had also provided a psychological cement that helped bind together French and English Canadians. For though its site was Montreal, Expo was still a Canadian affair, a part of a national celebration and the result of cooperation among all Canadians. If English and French Canadians could work together to produce Expo, perhaps they could also find a way to achieve a resolution of their long-lasting political enmity.

SEPARATIST RALLY draws a crowd of students to the snowy Concourse Place Ville Marie in Montreal in 1963. Brandishing Quebec's flag, the students protested discrimination against French Canadians in the assignment of top jobs in the Canadian National Railways, whose president they burned in effigy. By 1968 the railways had three French Canadian vice presidents.

New Ideas amid Settled Ways of Life

For two centuries the people of Quebec have felt themselves a neglected minority lost in the midst of a vast, fast-growing and English-speaking North America. Understandably, they have developed a system of defensive attitudes. Quebec to them was an island of agrarian simplicity in a sea of crass modernity. Change of every sort was to be resisted in favor of the "glorious past." Yet in 1960 change *did* come—with a new and forward-looking provincial government and a fresh enthusiasm for progress among intellectuals. Although Quebec still looks, and feels, quite different from the rest of North America, it shows promise of moving into the mainstream of the 20th Century.

INTENSE DISCUSSION engrosses five Quebec intellectuals who meet regularly at the Montreal home of Normand Hudon, a caricaturist and cartoonist *(second from right),* to thrash out their province's dilemmas. The bearded man is Abbé Ambroise Lafortune, who produces a television show and has written 12 books. The others include an author, a critic and a teacher.

yet enter more fully into the modern world

RESPECTED NEWSMAN, Claude Ryan, Director of the influential French daily *Le Devoir,* argues for a confederation in which Quebec is given ample powers. He opposes separatism.

VOICE OF SEPARATISM, former television commentator, war correspondent and Quebec cabinet minister René Lévesque has a dynamism that has attracted French Canadian youth.

OUTSPOKEN PRELATE, Monseigneur Maurice Roy, Quebec's archbishop and chancellor of Laval University, has rebuked the conservative clergy and helped modernize Laval's curriculum.

A RURAL FAMILY, the Simards retain a French Canadian closeness and piety even as Quebec changes

DEVOTED WIFE, Mme. Simard prepares Sunday breakfast for her husband, Edmond-Louis Simard, who maintains the family farm and is the benevolent ruler of the growing Simard clan.

At a supper to celebrate the baptism of a grandson, M. and Mme. Simard laugh with their guests as one of their daughters serves.

FACTORY WORKER, Régean Simard helps smooth the top of a cement block in a plant at Bagotville. More and more of Quebec's young men are leaving the land for industrial jobs.

PERSEVERING FARMERS, M. Simard and his third son, Laurier, plow one of their fields *(left)* with their team. Laurier is the only one of five sons to remain on the farm with his father.

Gathered for the baptism, the Simard children and their husbands and wives crowd around Mme. Simard to see the baptismal cake.

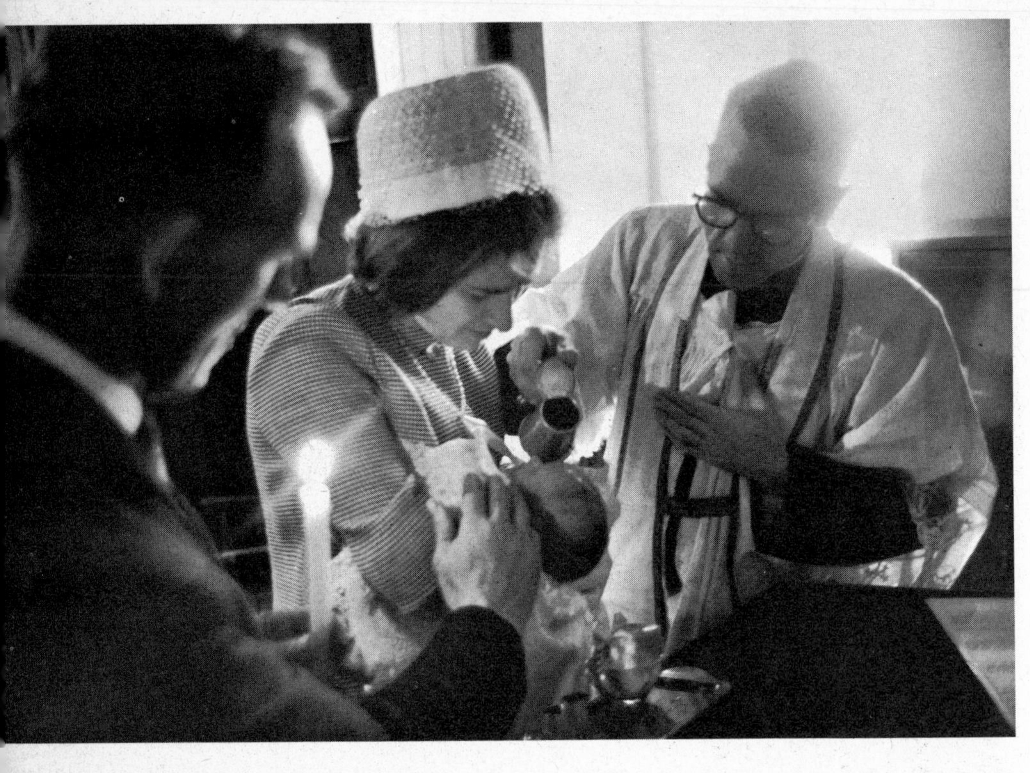

SOLEMN BAPTISM is administered by the parish priest to Laurier Simard's son, Louis, while his proud grandfather looks on. Like most of the people of Quebec, the Simards are pious Roman Catholics.

WEEKLY RENDEZVOUS of the Simard family takes place before Sunday Mass as they gather by their cars outside the strikingly modern church of St.-Marc de Bagotville. The church was completed in 1956.

TEACHING NUN confronts a lively, interested class of uniformed girls in a new classroom of the school built adjacent to the Bagotville church. Most education in Quebec is provided by Church schools.

A sled driver and his team of Huskies, the dogs resting at left, brace against a blizzard as it roars through a grove of Arctic firs.

The driver was heading for Padlei in the Northwest Territories.

7

The Empty Half of a Nation

IN the winter of 1947, a trapper named Shaback, lying in a makeshift shack in the Canadian Northwest Territories, made this entry in his diary: 43rd day without food. The previous September, finding little game and fearing starvation, he had begun to walk down the Caribou River toward civilization. But now, weakened by hunger, he had holed up in an empty shack. Awkwardly, he carved three words on a piece of wood, went out into the 30°-below-zero cold, nailed the piece of wood on the door of his shack and went inside again.

Over a year later, a half-breed trapper found the shack and noticed the piece of wood nailed to the door. On it Shaback had written: DEAD MAN HERE.

This story illustrates two important and abiding truths about the North. First it is a reminder that riches will always tempt men to dare this wilderness. Secondly, although it recalls the North of the gold rush era, it happened in our own times and could still happen today. For Canada's North, even in the space age, remains largely uninhabited and remote. Men may plant flags, draw maps and spell out its emptiness with names. But the mere rituals of possession remain as futile as the boast of a child who climbs on a sand dune to announce that now he is king of the castle. The sea does not hear the child; the snows do not know man is there. They remain indifferent.

And yet, for all its harsh terrain, the Canadian North has always exercised a mysterious and compelling attraction for men and women from all walks of life. Like the great desert, which similarly promises death for the unwary, it is a place which, once visited, invites return. Few who have stood among the isolated buildings of an arctic settlement, watching the plane—their only link aside from radio with the outside world—circle and disappear in the skies, have escaped the twin feelings of elation and fear which the Arctic inspires. The elation comes from that strange sense of peace which inhabits the wilderness. The fear is that, day after day, one will wait in vain for the plane's life-giving return. Man is an interloper in this place where death is constant—dead earth, dead snows and a cold that kills.

YET, again and again, one meets with people who were sent into the North on a summer job or under military orders and who, despite the loneliness and the bleakness, are eager to return. Questioned as to why, they are inarticulate in the manner of lovers. "It's just different," they say and smile uncomfortably.

Nor is this simply a national infatuation with a strange and unknown part of the homeland, for in the far north a visitor will discover German guides, British pilots, Swiss trappers, American prospectors and French missionaries, men whose lonely huts may contain the works of Goethe, the plays of Aeschylus and Sophocles or a learned treatise on Khmer art. Most of these men do not consider themselves immigrants and have little interest in the country called Canada. Apart from the missionaries, they are romantics who have simply turned their backs on civilization.

The missionaries, usually Anglican priests from England or Roman Catholic priests from France, are, of course, different. They came for souls and they are patient men. Two priests, discovered in an Indian settlement where they had built a church and a school, cheerfully admitted that they had lived there 10 years but had not made a single convert. A visitor asked if they were discouraged. "Discouraged?" said one of the Fathers. "Why? What is ten years in the history of the Church?"

POSSIBLY, in the past, this unhurried, low-pressure attitude toward life constituted a large part of the North's attraction for nonconformists and eccentrics. The blank, snowy wastes, the great distances still induce a womb-like feeling of security from the harsh pressures of the outside world. "A lot of people up here just wouldn't make it on the Outside," a Northern Affairs officer told a visitor. "Some work hard, others do as little as possible. Either way, nobody pays any attention to them. Living here can be the perfect escape hatch."

Yet feelings of depression are common to all who live in the Canadian North. In the journals of explorers, as in the letters home of ordinary settlers in small company towns, the same symptoms recur. Sudden irritability, sudden depressions are the rule. "Every settlement gets to think of itself as the end of the line," says a veteran RCMP constable. "Whether you're living with fifty Eskimos, a hundred Indians, or half a dozen technicians on a DEW [Distant Early Warning] Line station, that's your whole world. There's no sense of community with other settlements. They're too far away."

And so, there are times when everyone who lives in the North feels "bushed," and a trip to the South seems the only cure. Northern residents look on the "Outside" with a mixture of hatred and longing. It's a nice place to visit, but they no longer want to live there. They are glad to come back to their bleak, empty home.

Nowhere else in the world, except possibly in the Sahara desert and in Antarctica, are so few people settled in such an enormous block of land. The Northwest and Yukon Territories, which make up the bulk of the Canadian North, occupy a total area of one-and-a-half-million square miles. This is, roughly, 40 per cent of the total area of Canada. Yet only about 45,000 people live there. When one considers that this tiny population includes about 4,000 fulltime government workers, several thousand Indians and most of Canada's 13,000 Eskimos, it will be seen that the North has hardly been settled at all. Yet this is both natural and inevitable considering Canada's small population, lack of funds, and the geographic and climatic limitations of the Canadian North. In fact, in view of the limited means at their disposal it is remarkable that Canadians know as much as they do about various phases of Arctic research.

For, while Canada's universities and privately financed institutes have done excellent work with limited funds, all evidences point to the conclusion that Canada's North can only be fully exploited by the expenditure of billions of dollars and by a population in urgent need of living room. Russia's Far North, the most highly developed northern region in the world, has benefited from just such an infusion of men and money. Its population numbers about six million.

BUT Russia's Far North has, of course, great geographical advantages over Canada's North. While Canada has only one major arctic waterway, the Mackenzie, Russia has nine rivers of comparable importance, which run like parallel fingers of a hand down through its great arctic region. Not only do these rivers water fertile regions, but their outflow breaks the sea ice in spring and softens the climate. Parts of the Siberian Arctic were discovered and explored as far back as the 14th Century. Orders to explore the northern seacoast, from the White Sea to the farthest Siberian cape, were issued by the Russian government 40 years before the English explorer Samuel Hearne reached the Arctic Ocean overland across Canada at the mouth of the Coppermine River in 1772.

In addition, ever since the days of the czars, exiles have been made to settle in the Russian and Siberian northlands. After the 1917 Revolution, the Soviets, more interested in prestige than in profits, poured huge sums into their Far North, adopted long-range programs for educating the native peoples and in 1920 set up an Arctic Scientific Research Institute which now has a staff of 1,100, in contrast to similar Western institutes which usually function with staffs of a few dozen people. By 1958, more than 1,900 collective farms had been established in the Russian north, and there is a large complex of laboratories and military installations.

SIMILARLY, the U.S. state of Alaska points up the thinness of the population of Canada's far north. There are more than 145,000 people living in greater Anchorage, well over three times as many as live in the 1.5 million square miles of the Northwest and Yukon Territories. However, like Russia, Alaska possesses considerable geographical advantages over most of the Canadian North. Alaska's interior is forbidding enough, but much of its coast is warmed by the Japan Current of the Pacific and lends itself to lumbering, fishing and agriculture. Again, like Russia, Alaska has benefited from a massive infusion of government men and money. Its population almost doubled during World War II when the U.S. armed forces, engaged in fighting Japan, discovered its strategic importance. In the two decades of Cold War since 1945 the population has almost doubled again to its present level of about 272,000. A good deal of the recent increase is due to private enterprise, but much of Alaska's economy is still dependent on the government. Currently about half of the total employment in Alaska arises from various government activities, including the maintenance of navy and air force installations.

In contrast to Alaska and the Russian Far North, most of Canada's Northern regions were neatly, if facetiously, described by Superior Court Judge John H. Sissons of the Northwest Territories who said that in five days the good Lord made the earth and all the creatures on it; then on the sixth day He made the Northwest Territories; that done, on the seventh He sat back and threw rocks at it.

The extreme climatic and geographical rigor of the Canadian North goes far toward explaining why so few people, compared with either Alaska or Russia's Far North, live there. So does the fact that Canada's total population of 20 million is hardly more than one twelfth of Russia's 233 million. Canada simply does not have the people or the economic power to support massive development programs on the Russian model. Even with its large military expenditures, the U.S. has hardly begun to settle or develop Alaska.

THE story of Canada's development of its North, then, can be summed up fairly accurately in one sentence: where there are profits, there are people. Yellowknife, the capital city of the Northwest Territories and the site of one of the world's ranking gold mines, has a population of 4,500; a two-million-dollar high school, six churches, hotels and even a General Motors automobile agency. And if gold built Yellowknife, then furs built Aklavik (in Eskimo: The Place Where the Bear Crossed), which was begun in 1912 on the permanently frozen (permafrost) soil on the west channel of the Mackenzie River. Aklavik's houses unfortunately showed a tendency to sink into the permafrost when it had been melted by the heat of their floors. After some years it was decided to build a new settlement on the east channel of the river. Canadian government planners stepped in and helped build a showpiece town, named Inuvik (The Place of the Man). With its neat rows of bungalows built on stilts to avoid melting the permafrost and serviced by connecting sewage and water tunnels, also above ground, Inuvik is proof that living in a modern Northern settlement can be as comfortable as in a town in Southern Ontario. For, unlike the romantic foreigners who live in the far north to escape civilization, the new breed of Canadian company employees who live in the North's new towns have no desire to rough it. "In the future," says a Northern Affairs planner, "our towns will have shopping centers, bowling alleys and real paved streets. Just like any place else."

DESPITE the government's help in building Inuvik, most Northern experts agree that the creation of future model towns will depend on the discovery and profitable marketing of mineral resources in Northern regions. Rankin Inlet, where Eskimos were taught to be miners and mechanics with startling success, was a thriving community until the vein of nickel in its mine gave out. Uranium built a boom town on Great Bear Lake, but when the world market for uranium shrank, the boom town began to die. In certain areas new boom towns are on the way. Iron ore discoveries have brought 3,500 residents, cement sidewalks, a town swimming pool and four-family apartment houses to Labrador City in the cold, bleak wastes of western Labrador.

But though private companies and prospectors have mapped and claimed huge mineral deposits in many areas of the Canadian North, including northern Quebec and Labrador, these rich areas remain largely undeveloped. Similarly, in the arctic islands oil reserves of 21 billion barrels have been estimated, but a Canadian expert has warned that a billion dollars must be spent before this oil can reach markets in Eastern Canada and Europe. In most cases, therefore, the North's rich mineral reserves will remain untapped until road or rail communications can be brought in. Progress has been made along these lines both by government and by private industry, but a full-scale exploitation of the North's riches would involve staggering and, for the present, prohibitive initial costs. In the meantime, many of the communications services which do exist are provided by trading stations, supply vessels and aircraft of the Hudson's Bay Company in the huge territories which it once held under a royal charter.

"The Bay," as the company is known across Canada, set the pattern for the private interests which exploited the North. British-owned, it has long been associated in Canadian memories with an image of a vast, autocratic private state that reaped huge profits by paying the Eskimos minimum prices for their furs, defended its stake-outs with its own armed men and was the real ruler of Canada's Northern territories. One of the great sights of the early 1800s was the departure of a company chief factor on his annual inspection tour to the salute of a salvo of guns from the company's main fort, dressed as a contemporary observer put it, ". . . every day in a suit of black or dark blue, white shirt, collars to his ears, frock coat, velvet stock. . . . [and] a black beaver hat worth forty shillings. When travelling in a canoe or boat, he was lifted in or out by the crew. . . ."

The Bay has moved with the times: one of its store managers at present is an Eskimo and, while it still maintains 28 stores, many above the Arctic Circle, its Northern operations account for only a tiny fraction of its income. Its trading posts in the Prairies have blossomed into big department stores, and it is now Canada's third largest retailer, sells its own brands of Scotch whiskey and has moved into the oil business. Its renting of oil leases in the huge areas on which it holds oil and mineral rights now replaces the money it once made from renting out land. But the Bay is still the Bay: although the government is now in charge of most legal and welfare services, Bay managers in remote arctic outposts are still called on to settle Eskimo family quarrels, and the company continues its traditional trade with fur trappers.

THE trappers are tough, but they no longer are rugged individualists, paddling their own canoes downriver. For one thing, the canoe is likely to be made of fiber glass and powered by the latest in outboard motors. Even the Mounties, those staples of romantic Northern fiction, are less likely to be mushing their dog sleds across the barrens in relentless pursuit of their man than to be filling in a government form in a cozy modern substation. While the Mounties still police most Northern areas, their duties, apart from arresting the odd trapper or Indian for drunkenness or theft, are mainly those of roll keepers and game wardens.

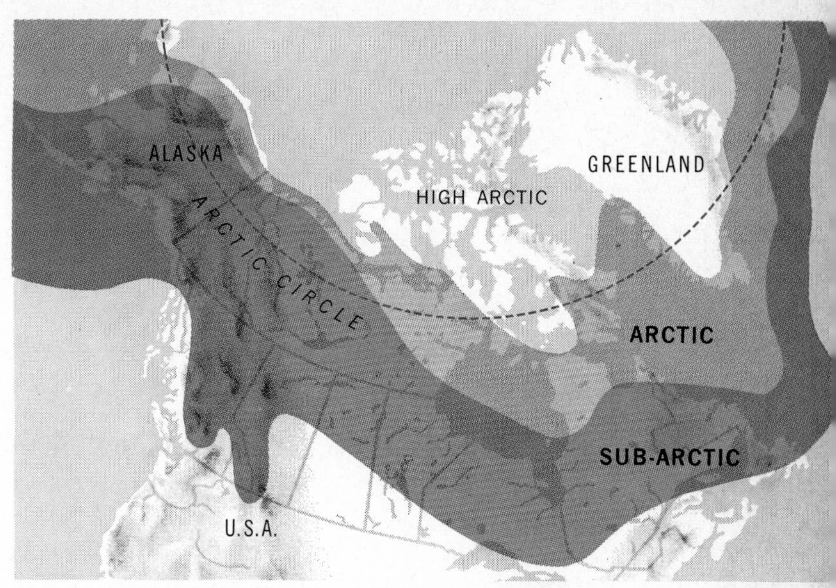

REGIONS OF THE NORTH consist of the Subarctic, which covers much of southern Canada (and even reaches into the U.S.); the Arctic; and, within the Arctic, the barren, icy high Arctic.

Most Eskimos no longer live in snow igloos, and their nomadic way of life is fast disappearing. Aided by Northern Affairs officials, the Eskimos are setting up cooperative retail trading stores which they themselves run, often in direct competition with the Bay, and producer cooperatives for the marketing of Eskimo carvings, toys and prints as well as fish and furs. Many Eskimos have been converted to Christianity, but they often retain elements of their old animistic religion. (An Eskimo hunter may still change his name if he has a bad hunting season, in hopes that evil spirits will not recognize him in his new guise.) Engaging and cheerful, they remain true sons of the Arctic and, as such, are the favorite wards of civil servants and Northern welfare workers. Cynics have said that it would be cheaper for the government to house Canada's total Eskimo population in the swank Chateau Laurier Hotel in Ottawa than it is to maintain the present Eskimo welfare services in the Arctic.

There are 218,000 Indians in Canada, and some 8,000 of them live in the North. Like the Eskimos, they are traditionally hunters and fishermen. Unlike them, they are not always cheerful and agreeable and have little respect or liking for government men, a feeling that seems to be reciprocated in Ottawa. While documentary films, pamphlets and photographs abound on the Eskimo and his habits, there is little information about the Indians, many of whom live an equally difficult and hazardous life—although the majority of Indians make their home in the regions below the timber line.

These lands differ greatly from the Arctic yet are a true part of Canada's North. In reality, the North is made up of three great regions, with considerable differences in climate and character. Farthest north is the high Arctic, a barren landscape totally hostile to man, a land which a geographer who mapped a part of it described as "looking as if some great claw had dug down out of the heavens and scratched deep gouges across its bleak surface." It is a land of terrible cold, of icy winds which men cannot bear. On a cold and windy winter day, a man going out improperly clothed might well freeze to death in 30 seconds. It is a land virtually deserted by the sun through long winter months, a territory shunned even by the Eskimos. Most geographers believe it can never be settled.

IMMEDIATELY below the high Arctic is the Arctic proper, where the mean temperature of the warmest month is never above 50° and winter temperatures may go as low as 80° below zero. Yet the example of Russia shows that large communities do exist in similar regions, and, as minerals, oil and natural gas have been discovered in the Arctic, planners foresee a day when large communities will settle there to mine these riches.

The tree line which meanders sometimes north of the Arctic Circle, sometimes south of it, divides the true Arctic from the subarctic region beneath it. Despite the fact that this region reaches southward to such comparatively moderate climes as southern Alberta, the subarctic areas of the North are still brutally cold in the winter. The mercury does go above 50° in the summer but only for four months at the most, while average January temperatures may dip to 36° below zero. Yet in the brief Northern summers, cabbages big as basketballs, dahlias like soup plates, and carrots a foot long spring from the thin, unfrozen layer of soil.

FORT SMITH, which lies a little south of Great Slave Lake in the Northwest Territories, has an all-time summer high of 103°, which, the locals boast, is 1° higher than the highest recorded temperature in New Orleans. They do not boast of the −70° low that has been registered on the western edge of their region in the wintertime. And while planners talk enthusiastically of the almost 24 hours of uninterrupted summer sunlight in this land of the midnight sun, they are discreet about the swarms of black flies and mosquitoes it attracts. In fact, only in the Queen Elizabeth Islands in the high Arctic is the summer visitor spared the attentions of these twin arctic pests.

The subarctic remains the chief hope of those Canadians who dream of a Northern Empire, for it can be settled should enough mineral resources be discovered to make this profitable. Yet, as in the Arctic proper, the initial cost would be staggering. Much of the area is covered with muskeg—spongy, odoriferous swampland impassable save when frozen in winter. In warmer weather it swallows up all the roads and railroad tracks man tries to lay upon it. This oozy pest, as much as the cold and the vast distances, is responsible for the fact that as late as 1966 there were only 200 miles of railroads in the mineral rich Northwest and Yukon Territories. In the whole area there were less than 3,000 miles of roads, most of them with gravel surfaces. Elsewhere in the North, conditions are similar. Local roads rarely interconnect. They run a few miles, then end.

Many of the large developments and some of the communications which exist in the North today were developed by private companies. A U.S.-Canadian combine pushed a 357-mile private railroad from the Quebec fishing port of Sept-Iles north to mine sites in remote Ungava, where iron ore deposits have been found that may rival the once-great American Mesabi Range. Crest Exploration Ltd., a subsidiary of Standard Oil of California, has completed an extensive survey of iron ore possibilities on the border of the Yukon and Northwest Territories. Crest holds iron ore claims covering 78,800 acres about 290 miles northeast of Whitehorse. The company has built an airstrip at the site and has made a study of the feasibility of constructing a railroad into the area. At Carol Lake in Labrador, a U.S.-Canadian combine has built a $65-million plant that turns iron ore concentrate into high-grade pellets.

While all these efforts count in developing this huge area, few companies have the resources to embark on multimillion-dollar development programs which may take 10 to 20 years to show up as a profit on company ledgers. In addition, it is most doubtful that, with Canada's present economic difficulties, any government could obtain popular support for costly long-range federal development programs. Nevertheless, there is a feeling abroad in Canada that more must be done to develop the North. Canadian federal investment in the Northwest and Yukon Territories was barely more than one per cent of the national budget in 1966-1967, and in the same period the province of Quebec, which administers its own northern regions, spent about the same proportion of its annual budget on them.

DEVELOPED or not, the North remains all-important to the Canadians' self-image. It makes their country the second largest on earth. Its promise of riches is a lottery in which every Canadian holds a ticket, yet at the same time it is a reminder of the frontier past, of a simpler and purer world into which he may still escape. Above all, its brooding physical presence over the land is a warning that Canadians have not yet conquered their universe. "But look at the big picture!" cries an excited article in *North*, a government-sponsored arctic magazine. "See how far the north has come, look at it now, imagine where it's going! Is it possible, do you suppose, that even [the late Arctic explorer Vilhjalmur] Stefansson, the optimist and visionary, underestimated the worth of the place? Can't you smell the gold lying there, around the next bend in the river, through the next pass in the mountains?"

Undoubtedly, the gold, silver, nickel, lead, zinc, iron, oil and natural gas are all there. Perhaps in future decades a combination of public and private interests, both in Canada and abroad, will combine to produce the huge numbers of men and dollars necessary to unlock this arctic treasure chest. When, and if, that comes to pass, Canada may fulfill the prediction made by Disraeli in 1846 and at last become "the Russia of the New World."

CANADA'S RENOWNED MOUNTED POLICE

Entrusted today with a multitude of law enforcement tasks, the "Mounties" were originally formed as the North West Mounted Police almost a century ago to keep order in the Indian hunting grounds in the West. They were charged primarily with reducing strife among the Indians and protecting them from swindling fur traders. They adopted scarlet tunics because the scarlet uniforms of the British army were regarded by the Indians as symbols of courage and fair dealing.

AFTER HEROIC SERVICE in the West, the renamed Royal Canadian Mounted Police was given a vastly expanded role in Canadian police work. Today the Mounties are the law enforcement arm of the federal government, with duties similar to those of America's FBI. They look out for narcotics traffic, income-tax evasion and a host of other crimes. In addition, they are Canada's intelligence agency, responsible for detecting espionage and subversion. In all the provinces except Quebec and Ontario, the RCMP functions as provincial as well as federal police.

IN THE FAR NORTH the Mounties are the sole police force, and there they still occasionally fulfill the romantic vision of rugged men mushing through blizzards on dog sleds. They are more likely to travel by airplane, however, as they maintain 41 detachments in the Northwest and Yukon Territories.

DEDICATED JUDGE, the late John H. Sissons of the Northwest Territories *(foreground)* presides at a trial on Baffin Island. He made semiannual tours of his vast area.

A Slow Battle to Develop a Frozen Domain

Few people realize the enormous size of the Canadian North. Baffin Island is alone as large as Ohio, Pennsylvania, New York and all of New England put together. And few realize the extreme rigor of the climate. Much of Canada's North lies above the tree line, where nothing grows except Arctic plants and where snow covers the ground nine months of the year. The Queen Elizabeth Islands stretch so far north that Commodore Robert Peary used one of them, Ellesmere Island, as his jumping-off place in 1909, when he became the first man to reach the Pole. But men do live in this inhospitable land. Drawn once by the abundance of valuable furs, they now go to mine the minerals that underlie the tundra. As the earth's accessible storehouses of minerals are exhausted, more and more men will brave Canada's rugged North.

MODEL TOWN of Inuvik in the Mackenzie River delta, raised on stilts so the buildings' heat will not melt the permafrost, cost the government $34 million to build.

RADAR STATIONS of the DEW Line scan the Arctic skies from frozen promontories all across the Canadian North

ISOLATED OUTPOST at Cape Dyer on Baffin Island thrusts its radar and radio equipment above a seemingly infinite landscape of ice and snow. Winter temperatures may fall to 65° below zero.

MASSIVE REFLECTOR at Cape Dyer bounces radio waves from an antenna *(foreground)* into the troposphere, where they are reflected back to defense control centers in Canada and the U.S.

NORTHERN NATIVES, the Eskimos are surprisingly adaptable to modern ways

PICKING BERRIES, Eskimo girls from a tribe that still lives by hunting pause during a search for firewood *(opposite)* to consume one of the few edibles provided by their tundra home.

MINING NICKEL at Rankin Inlet, Eskimo workers descend into the mine's deep shaft. Eskimos have become expert miners, mechanics and industrial workers with only minimal training.

Eskimos chat in the general store at Rankin Inlet. The Eskimos often buy refrigerators—which they use to keep food from freezing.

TRANSPLANTED STUDENTS from a forestry school in Hungary hear a lecture on the timber of Canada's West. They are some of the 291 forestry students and teachers who fled Hungary in 1956 and entered the University of British Columbia.

The Immigrant Tide

IN 1939, when George VI, the first reigning British monarch to visit Canada, arrived for his one and only royal tour, the nation was prostrate in its devotion and enthusiasm. A forest of Union Jacks appeared at every whistle-stop, and faces shone with patriotic joy when military bands played *God Save the King*.

Eighteen years later, in 1957, when King George's daughter, Queen Elizabeth II, arrived to open the Canadian Parliament, Gallup pollsters crossed the country to find out what people thought of her coming. Sixty-three per cent of the Canadians polled were either indifferent or openly critical of the visit. At about this time, a poll of Canada's high-school students showed that an overwhelming majority wanted a new national flag. Less than 13 per cent voted to retain the Union Jack for ceremonial use. And when, a year after Elizabeth's opening of Parliament in 1957, the Canadian government was asked to foot the bill for another visit, this time a full-dress, coast-to-coast royal tour, many people began to grumble.

Yet Elizabeth is, officially, Queen of Canada and this was only her third visit to her realm. (She made her first cross-country visit, as princess, in 1951.) In 1959, during the third tour, letters poured in to the Toronto *Star,* one of the few newspapers critical of the visit, complaining about the high cost of these royal junkets, the useless formal ceremonies involved and the snobbish hauteur of the Queen's entourage. By the time the tour was over, some officials prophesied that the country would never have another. In the future, it was said, royalty would be invited only for specific ceremonial jobs, such as laying a cornerstone or attending a centenary celebration. On just such a ceremonial visit in 1964, the Queen was greeted in Quebec by a mixture of indifference and rudeness, with rowdy young Separatists crying, "Shoo, shoo, shoo."

ALL this profoundly puzzled Canada's Establishment. And there were other odd portents. When, for example, during the tour of 1959, the Queen crossed the border and visited Chicago, she met a tumultuous welcome, more spontaneous than any shown her in Canada. What did it all mean? Were the polls right about public apathy? Why were there so many rude complaints in the letters to the newspapers? More recently, were the small crowds in Quebec really a sign of indifference or the result of fear that fanatical Separatists might hurl a bomb? These questions were quietly discussed in Ottawa and in the leathery gloom of English Canada's clubs. Disgusted Anglophiles tended to blame much of the apathy toward the 1959 tour on "those foreigners" who had entered Canada in such numbers since World War II. It was felt that their answers had probably influenced the Gallup poll. "Foreigners," it was said, had no feeling for the Crown as Canada's unifying link.

In reality, it seems unlikely that new immigrants, confronted by an official-sounding polltaker, would announce any indifference they might feel toward the Queen's visit. For, curiously enough, a new Canadian citizen is asked to pledge allegiance not to Canada but to "Queen Elizabeth II, her heirs and successors." Those who went on record against the visit were largely second- or third-generation Canadians like Joyce Davidson, a CBC television interviewer, who came under heavy criticism for her statement on a U.S. television program that she was "indifferent" to the Queen's coming, or June Callwood, a Canadian journalist, who, commenting on the reception prepared by Chicago for the Queen's visit, wrote in *Look* Magazine: "Americans can afford to cheer themselves hoarse over the Queen without any second thoughts about what she symbolizes." To Miss Callwood, and many other native-born Canadians, the Queen symbolizes "the apron strings that Canada long ago discarded."

However, the Anglophiles who blamed the ambivalent attitudes toward the royal tour on "those foreigners" were at least partly right. Non-British immigrants have been entering Canada in large numbers since the middle of the 19th Century. The exodus of Germans to Canada's Prairie provinces had reached such proportions by 1905 that the Wilhelmstrasse protested to London that "the attempt to lure our fellow countrymen to this desert subarctic region is to be denounced as criminal." Yet the Germans kept coming. John Diefenbaker, prime minister of Canada at the time of Queen Elizabeth's 1959 tour, was himself partly of German descent.

Since World War II, close to three million immigrants have entered Canada and almost two thirds of them are from countries that do not have English as their native tongue. Britons and Italians have for many years been the two largest annual immigrant groups, alternating for the top spot depending on the changing prosperity and employment situations in the two countries.

AS for the French Canadians, Canada's second largest national group, their numbers have not significantly increased through immigration from France. Only 73,541 French immigrants entered Canada between 1946 and 1967. The French Canadian attitude toward "New Canadians" was summed up by the late Henri Bourassa, a nationalist leader who charged that the purpose of federal immigration policies was to swamp the French minority in a sea of foreign "drunkards, paupers, loafers and jailbirds," and that special cheap transcontinental railroad fares for immigrants made it "more expensive for an inhabitant of Rivière-du-Loup to go to Alberta than for a Jew from Galicia or a peasant from the Danube." When a wartime French collaborator named Count Jacques de Bernonville, under sentence of death in France for helping the Nazis, was discovered hiding in Montreal, French Canadian politicians and editors protested the government's decision to deport "a Frenchman, a Catholic and a patriot," while "ruffians, scoundrels and Communist Riffraff" were being admitted.

UNDER these circumstances, it is not surprising that the majority of European immigrants wish to embrace the reigning English-speaking culture and send their children to English-speaking schools. But Canada's school system was not designed, as was America's, to inculcate patriotism in the children of the foreign born. The majority of immigrant children had, traditionally, been the offspring of British families who tended to think of England as "home" and presumed that English institutions were the model for Canadian ones. Canadian schools have never been imbued with the pride in national achievements, ideals and history which is so evident in U.S. teaching programs.

The American school-assembly custom of saluting the flag and singing a patriotic song is practiced in many Canadian schools. But harmony is not complete, for Canadians have yet to agree on an official version out of 26 existing English texts sung to the tune of their national anthem *O Canada*. The French words of *O Canada* please the French but are considered a "Papist French folk song" by Loyalist Protestant Canadians. *God Save the Queen* remains an official Canadian anthem to be sung on royal occasions, though many Canadians choke on it. If neither of these seems safe, bands will strike up *The Maple Leaf Forever*, an uninspired and virtually unsingable jingle. Few Canadian schoolchildren can rattle off a list of the country's prime ministers the way U.S. schoolchildren recite the former presidents, and training courses for immigrants tend to be practical rather than ideological in scope.

Nevertheless, over the years, a large proportion of the European immigrants and their children have developed a strong patriotic feeling toward their new country. Unlike many British immigrants, they have accepted Canada wholly and enthusiastically, with no colonial reservations that its ways are provincial or inferior to those of Britain. They have become more and more Canadian—a new breed of Canadian—as they have been assimilated into the English-speaking community. Today, despite the fact that persons of British descent still outnumber all other nationalities in six provinces—Newfoundland, Prince Edward Island, Nova Scotia, New Brunswick, Ontario and British Columbia—Canada is no longer, as the Fathers of Confederation planned it, a British nation with a French minority. More than one quarter of the present population belongs to other ethnic groups.

THESE groups have won a voice in Canada's affairs. Members of the federal Parliament have included Ukrainians, Italians, Belgians, a Pole, an Icelander, a Lebanese and men of Swedish, German, Norwegian and Chinese ancestry. Descendants of Danes, Ukrainians, Icelanders, Norwegians, Swedes and Germans have been ministers of provincial governments. Men of the Jewish faith have been elected mayors of several Canadian cities. Ukrainians have held similar office in Winnipeg, Edmonton and Fort William. Ukrainians, Russians, Icelanders and Lebanese hold seats in Canada's Senate, and in 1961 Louis Rasminsky was appointed governor of the Bank of Canada—a position that makes him watchdog of the country's monetary policy. It is the highest post in government ever obtained by a Canadian Jew.

Yet, until 1962, Canadian immigration policies were still dominated by the ostrich view of the late Prime Minister Mackenzie King, who announced after World War II that "the people of Canada do not wish, as a result of mass immigration, to make a fundamental alteration in the character of our population. . . ." Translated into official policy, this meant that Canada gave first preference to immigrants from Britain, France, the United States, Ireland, New Zealand, South Africa and Australia. Citizens of other lands were admitted only if the minister of citizenship and immigration deemed them "desirable future citizens," not liable to "give rise to social and economic problems."

THUS equipped with almost absolute powers, Canadian ministers of immigration were able to decide that people from Northwestern Europe were more desirable than Eastern or Southern Europeans and that even Commonwealth citizens were not desirable if they were colored British West Indians, Asians or citizens of India. It meant that in the postwar years more than a quarter of a million Germans were admitted to Canada without any plebiscite or discussion as to whether they might "make a fundamental alteration" in the character of the population. It meant that the minister of immigration could admit 7,709 Poles in 1952 and decide that only 2,870 should be admitted in 1953. To Canada's credit, it also meant that all screening regulations were waived to admit 37,566 Hungarian refugees in the two years after the 1956 revolt. This was a larger number than was taken by any other nation.

In pursuing exclusionary policies in its immigration system, Canada was following the practice of several other nations similarly faced with a large flow of would-be immigrants. Australia, Brazil and the United States included similar exclusionary provisions in their systems. However, many Canadians, while highly critical of U.S. immigration policies, remained unaware of the real situation in their own country.

Significantly, when these regulations were changed in 1962, the change came at the instigation of Douglas Jung, a Chinese-Canadian member of Parliament and a member of a race heavily discriminated against by the old laws. The new regulation abolishes the old system of preferred countries and "will lay primary stress on education, training and skills as the main conditions of admissibility, regardless of the country of origin of the applicant." Critics of the regulation point out that it still leaves the minister of immigration his old dictatorial power over who gets in and who stays in. It is, however, a declaration to the rest of the world that Canada is no longer a frontier country in the market for brute labor and hardy settlers, but a highly organized industrial society, desperately in need of foreign brains and skills.

But if Canada is to become a true land of opportunity where these brains and skills are justly rewarded, changes must occur in the country's social structure. In the past, as the Canadian historian A.R.M. Lower sourly remarks: "It has been our job to take in the immigrants, educate them and their children, train them in citizenship and then pass on the better, brighter and more energetic among them to their fuller destiny in the States. . . . To this aspect of migration, Canadian statesmanship, past and present, has been almost totally blind."

AN immigrant might answer this charge with the remark that it is precisely because Canada has not "trained them in citizenship" that the brighter among them tend to leave for their "fuller destiny" in the States. Canadians have long blamed the higher U.S. standard of living and greater job opportunities for the fact that so many immigrants to Canada—currently about 12,000 a year—move on south of the border. It has rarely occurred to Canadians that perhaps the feeling of nonbelonging which European immigrants feel in a land where those of English origin are strongly in the ascendancy has at least as much to do with this large-scale defection to the States as have higher U.S. wages and incentives. The very term "New Canadian" sums up Canadian ambivalence towards immigrants. In the United States immigrants do not go through life with this distinguishing title. When they become American citizens, they are Americans.

This unwillingness to examine the national attitudes toward minority groups is doubly dangerous today when, as the criticism of the royal tours seems to indicate, the British Crown no longer serves as the cement of nationalism and patriotism. To many observers, the Queen's postwar appearances on the Canadian scene merely emphasized the present gulf between Britain, where titles are the bludgeon of privilege used to maintain a social pecking order that is carefully graded down from dukes to dustmen, and Canada, whose frontier egalitarianism was summed up by an anonymous native bard at the time the Canadian government forbade its citizens to accept British titles. His doggerel ran:

Away with honors, knighthoods, swords;
In proof of high endeavour
We'll wear where Adam wore the fig
The Maple Leaf forever.

It is precisely this transatlantic irreverence which finds favor with Canada's immigrants. Even the more reserved among them are captivated by it. Leon Koerner, a Czech lumber millionaire who lost most of his huge fortune when he fled to Canada in 1939 to escape Hitler, set out with his brother to investigate lumber mills near Vancouver. The Koerners, who had always had a chauffeur in Europe, hired a big chauffeur-driven car and headed out into the forests of British Columbia. After a couple of hours of sightseeing, the man at the wheel turned around: "How about a beer?" he asked.

The Koerners were shocked. In all their lives a servant had never addressed them unless spoken to first. "We don't want a drink," Leon Koerner told the Canadian. "But please have one yourself." The driver promptly pulled in at a beer parlor, opened the back door of the car and said: "Aw, come on. Have a beer." Bewildered, the Koerners followed him inside. When the chauffeur insisted on paying—"I asked *you,* didn't I?"—they were speechless. Yet his lack of servility helped decide them to stay in Vancouver and open a mill. Today Leon Koerner is Vancouver's biggest philanthropist and has donated splendid new buildings to the University of British Columbia.

A ROSTER OF FAMOUS SCIENTISTS

Canada has been blessed with many outstanding scientists—some native born, others immigrants. Some have been doctors whose innovations have changed medicine the world over. A partial list of these scientists follows.

ALEXANDER GRAHAM BELL (1847-1922) emigrated to Canada from Scotland at the age of 23. In Brantford, Ontario, he did much of the research in electricity which led to his invention of the telephone, although he actually constructed the first telephone in Boston, Massachusetts. He built a home in Nova Scotia in 1892 where he carried on many of his later experiments.

SIR WILLIAM OSLER (1849-1919), born in Ontario, had a greater influence on modern medical practice than perhaps any other man. He is credited with being the first to perceive that many organic illnesses have psychological origins. Teaching at McGill, the University of Pennsylvania, Johns Hopkins and Oxford, he helped modernize medical training and taught such great doctors as the Mayo brothers and Harvey Cushing.

SIR FREDERICK BANTING (1891-1941), son of an Ontario farmer, won a Nobel Prize for his discovery that diabetes is caused by a lack of insulin. He was aided in his work by Dr. Charles H. Best, another Canadian.

WILDER GRAVES PENFIELD (1891-   ), an immigrant to Canada from America, is recognized as the greatest contributor to neurology and neurosurgery in recent times. He is an expert on epilepsy and has greatly increased man's knowledge of how the brain functions.

Koerner's achievement in becoming a multimillionaire all over again in Canada is typical of the successful Canadian immigrant, although, unlike most other newcomers, he started his new life with a considerable stock of capital. In the lumber camps he noticed that hemlock, a heavy wood which is difficult to ship and prone to warp, was despised by Canadian lumbermen except for pulp and paper. Using European methods, he treated the wood, renamed it Alaska pine and shipped it to his old European customers. His story is typical in that, like most successful immigrants, he did not try to compete directly with Canadians in their markets, preferring to find new uses for materials which had previously been overlooked. Similarly, Karl Meyer, a German immigrant, discovered that there were no shoe factories in

Alberta, which is the heart of Canada's cattle country. Meyer started a small family factory and made a fortune.

Adam Citron, a Pole, who landed in Canada with five dollars in his pocket and went to work as a garage mechanic, saw the damage which Canada's snow-filled and salt-encrusted streets did to automobile fenders. He developed a fiber glass replacement fender which will not rot or rust, and now he has a coast-to-coast business selling them. A Dutchman bought thousands of acres of black muck bog at bargain prices and turned them into a gigantic vegetable garden which sells its packaged produce throughout central Canada. A Venetian started a glass factory, a Dutchman a pickle factory, a Czech manufactures synthetic glues from European formulas to suit Canadian wood products—such stories of new riches crowd the columns of Canada's periodicals.

Less noticed by the press are the thousands of European technicians without whose skills Canada's hospitals and laboratories would be unable to function. Thousands of immigrants teach in Canadian universities and high schools. Montreal's McGill University has augmented its staff with scores of immigrant professors and research technicians, while the *Université de Montréal*'s most famous staff member is Dr. Hans Selye, an Austrian immigrant, internationally acclaimed for his theory of stress and his experiments to determine what part stress plays in such ills of our high pressure age as heart disease, ulcers and arthritis.

EUROPEAN immigrants also direct most of Canada's symphony orchestras. They founded two of the three large ballet companies. They have started three opera companies which have persuaded such Canadian immigrants as the former Czech basso Jan Rubes to sing with them. Second- and third-generation Jewish immigrants have produced a large group of poets and novelists, some of whom, like Mordecai Richler, Leonard Cohen, William Weintraub and Jack Ludwig, have brought a new iconoclastic note into Canadian fiction. Takao Tanabe and Kazuo Nakamura are among Canada's most accomplished young abstract painters. Both are of Japanese origin. Guido Molinari, another accomplished abstractionist, is of Italian origin. Marek Jablonski, who has been acclaimed as a pianist in the U.S. and in Europe, is a first-generation Pole. Danish-born Erica Deichmann is probably Canada's finest potter and has achieved an international reputation in her craft.

In short, the huge waves of immigration which followed both world wars have given Canada a rich transfusion of new blood. The country, as a result, is now irrevocably committed to a future in which minorities will play a more important role. The new immigration regulations have cleared the way for Canada to become a melting pot of nationalities in which brains and skills will be the criteria, both for admission and for eventual success.

BUT Canada's future as an independent nation demands that much more be done. The task facing new governments will be to prove to minorities—French Canadian, European and others—that the nation offers equal opportunities to all its citizens. To do this, and to satisfy the increasingly Americanized younger generation of English Canadians, Canada must devise a more fitting symbol of nationhood than its waning attachment to the British Crown. Future generations will not be content with a set of ceremonies, presided over by governors-general and governors-provincial, who represent the Queen, not Canada. For these ceremonies are borrowed from Britain and based on a class system which is nonexistent in Canada. There will be an increasing demand for a more egalitarian concept of citizenship, for this egalitarianism is not simply North American but is evident also in Australia, another restless dominion with a huge and frightening landscape which, in many ways, resembles Canada's. As this spirit grows stronger, the differences between Canadians and New Canadians should disappear. Then, perhaps, that century-old hemorrhage of brains and skills to points south of the border may abate.

Spanking-new buildings of modern design adorn the trim 1,000-acre campus of the University of British Columbia in Vancouver.

A Beckoning Land of Opportunity in the West

The great fertile plains of the Canadian Prairie provinces and the forests and fisheries of British Columbia have attracted droves of immigrants since they were opened up in the last century. Germans, Poles, Ukrainians and people from a dozen other European countries—as well as Canadians and Americans—streamed into this new, wide land of opportunity. They still do. Homesteads with enough acreage for profitable modern farming may still be had for amazingly small sums. The expanding oil and gas industries offer increasing employment and occasionally produce a millionaire. The Canadian West is one of the few places left where opportunity seems unlimited, where hard work seems sure to produce a good life and possibly a fortune.

WIDE FIELDS worked by giant machines make farming a profitable business

A FARM AUCTION attracts an interested crowd in Drake, Saskatchewan, as the auctioneer prepares to sell a massive planting machine, a type useful only on large farms.

FARMING COMMUNITY typical of the Prairies *(opposite)* huddles by the railroad that links the vast surrounding fields to markets in the East and on the West Coast.

HUNGRY BUYERS at the auction have a hefty snack served by local wives *(right)*. The farm's owner had made enough in 32 years of farming to retire to California.

SPACE-AGE CAMPUS of British Columbia's Simon Fraser University evokes the dynamism and optimism of the new West

COVERED WALKWAYS connecting Simon Fraser's buildings provide year-round protection from the elements. The University is named for the explorer who probed western Canada.

MASSIVE MALL is dominated by a huge roof of steel trusses. Established by the provincial government, the University in 1965 had 2,700 students. In 1967 it had more than 5,000.

HOMESTEADERS, the Bouck family struggles to fulfill their promise to improve the land they acquired from the government

DEEP FURROWS are cut in the virgin prairie by Jim Bouck's tractor-drawn harrow. Homesteaders can buy Crown land for the low price of about $10 a "quarter section," which is 160 acres.

ATTENTIVE FATHER, Jim Bouck washes the face of two-year-old Howard. The Bouck farm is near Bonanza, Alberta, in the Peace River area, a vast tract of Crown land now being settled.

NOONTIME MEAL is served Jim Bouck and young Howard by Jim's wife, Anita. The Boucks live in a large, well-equipped trailer which they hauled to Alberta and then put up on blocks.

FAMILY PATRIARCH Lee Bouck and his wife sit on the stoop of their trailer. All the Boucks—Lee, Jim and Jim's three brothers—moved together to adjoining homesteads in Alberta.

KITCHEN GARDEN is the province of Anita Bouck, who hoes a furrow while she minds Howard. Despite the arduous and lonely life, homesteading has attracted many Canadians to the West.

BC
CBC
2
CBC

A LECTURE ON ART is delivered before CBC television cameras by Kathleen M. Fenwick (in light suit), a curator of the National Gallery in Ottawa, as she converses with a moderator of a noted TV series devoted to cultural activities.

9

Clothes but No Emperor

A FEW years ago, Glenn Gould, the young Toronto pianist, returned from his triumphs in the United States to give a concert in Vancouver. Gould, whose platform manner is as eccentric as his playing is brilliant, discoursed lengthily on Bach as he sat on a special folding chair at his special "Bach piano" (a small grand with staples in the hammers), his own rug under his feet, wearing a suit of long underwear under his baggy tails (because he greatly fears the cold). As he wound up his dissertation by saying, ". . . the really essential thing about Bach is . . ." a voice from the balcony called out, ". . . is to *play* him."

Canadians today must feel much as did that put-upon Vancouver concertgoer. In the past 15 years, in search of a culture they can call their own, they have appointed royal commissions, attended lectures, raised money, invited consultants and, in the process, have suffered every humiliation known to the supplicant. They have been lectured, advised, warned and dismissed by a stream of professors, novelists, poets and pundits, many of them Americans or Britons, whose ignorance of Canada's problems has been matched only by their sublime condescension. Today, one could hardly blame the Canadians if they followed the counsel of

Hermann Goering, who is reputed to have said that when he heard the word "culture" he reached for his revolver. Instead, with remarkable patience, they continue their search.

This search has been spurred by the condescending attitude toward Canada of the three nations from whose cultures the country has borrowed. The French, who were first on the Canadian scene, continue to think of French Canada as merely a province of French culture. Novels, poems and paintings by French Canadians are published and exhibited in Paris as though they were made in France. In a way this is just, for French Canada has given birth to no truly indigenous art. (Incidentally, the most celebrated novel of French Canada, an account of rural Quebec life entitled *Maria Chapdelaine*, was written by an expatriate Frenchman named Louis Hémon. The most famous poem about French Canada is, of course, "Evangeline," by Henry Wadsworth Longfellow, an American.)

Traditionally, Quebec has followed the lead of France and has always held art and artists in high esteem. But, until the 1960s, books were rarely printed which might be considered offensive to the Roman Catholic Church. Similarly, editors, publishers, official curators and cultural-affairs officers were wary of sanctioning any art which might not meet with Church approval. This, however, has been changing. The Church is no longer so rigid in its views, and censorship is no longer stringent. The search for greater freedom and for a culture that does not rest solely on Catholic teachings now obsesses the younger French Canadian intellectuals: it is largely responsible for the gradual disassociation of Quebec's schools and colleges from clerical control.

ESCAPE from the narrow academicism which for many years characterized the art schools of Quebec toward the artistic freedom of Paris helped establish two French Canadians as leading figures in the international school of Abstract Expressionism. They are the late Paul-Emile Borduas, who died in Paris in 1960, and Jean-Paul Riopelle, who still lives there. They are the only Canadian painters who have great international reputations and, despite their prolonged absence from Canada, they have exercised an enormous influence on Quebec's younger painters.

French Canadian writers are similarly influenced by Paris. They keep up with French literary journals, much as would provincials from Rouen. American literature interests them hardly at all. Books by new American writers are rarely translated into French or read in Quebec. The same goes for the works of English Canadian writers. On the other hand, it is equally rare to see a French Canadian book translated into English. Among the few French Canadian writers with an international reputation are Gabrielle Roy, whose novel of Montreal poverty (published in the U.S. as *The Tin Flute*) won France's *Prix Femina* in 1947, and Marie-Claire Blais, who wrote about Quebec rural squalor in *A Season in the Life of Emmanuel*. The book won the prestigious French *Prix Médicis* in 1966 and was translated into a dozen languages.

UNTIL recently, a French Canadian writer had first to win acceptance in Paris before his work would really be accepted in Canada. But, with the rise of French Canadian nationalism, novels, poems and plays are now pouring off Quebec presses. Some books have sold as many as 125,000 copies in trade editions, a figure that would make them bestsellers in the United States, which has roughly 36 times the population of Quebec.

English Canadians, unlike the French, have not even been granted the privilege of assimilation by the mother country. The British, quite simply, refuse to consider Canada as a place where art is possible and, in the words of the *Manchester Guardian*, see the country as a "cultural backwater." Perhaps this is because so many Britons remember the judgment pronounced by England's Samuel Butler, the author of *The Way of All Flesh* and *Erewhon*, who, on a visit to Canada, wrote an angry poem berating the Victorian philistinism of Montreal's middle-class merchants with the memorable tag line: "O, God! O, Montreal!" Butler's rage was incited by his discovery that a Greek statue had been banished to a Montreal attic because, being trouserless, it was considered "indecent."

This view of Canada as a wasteland was echoed in 1963 by the poet W. H. Auden, who wrote that: "The Dominions . . . are for me *tiefste Provinz* [deepest hinterlands], places which have produced no art and are inhabited by the kind of person with whom I have least in common." The attachment of British lowbrows to the Commonwealth in preference to joining the European Common Market was, he said, because the dominions "are inhabited by . . . people like themselves, speaking English, eating English food, wearing English clothes and playing English games. . . ." J. B. Priestley, a bluff, journeyman British novelist, told English audiences on his return from a tour of Canada that Canadians are "frustrated" and urged that if there is not sufficient talent in Canada, then talent should be imported. He later wrote a play for the culture-starved Canadians, presumably as an example of the talent he felt they should import. It closed after 37 performances in Toronto. Similarly, the late playwright Brendan Behan, imported as a flower of Irish culture, announced, after a boozy rendezvous with the Canadian constabulary, that he held the country in very low esteem. His cultural ukase: "Ireland will put a shillelagh into orbit, Israel will put a matzo ball into orbit and Liechtenstein will put a postage stamp into orbit before you Canadians ever put up a mouse."

BUT perhaps it is better to be insulted than ignored. American influence on Canadian art, while relatively new, is the most immediate and encompassing of all. Yet it would seem that, for Americans, Canadian art does not exist. Even the knowing American viewer of a Riopelle painting in New York's Museum of Modern Art tends to think of the artist as a Parisian, not a native of Montreal. Nor do the thousands of concertgoers who pack Manhattan's Town Hall to hear the glorious contralto of Maureen Forrester think of her as a Canadian, born and brought up in Montreal. She seems the most American of divas. The avant-garde cinema compositions of Canada's Norman McLaren (he draws directly on film, sending weird shapes and colors dancing across the screen) have won him the raves of American cinema buffs. Yet very few Americans have visited Montreal to study his techniques.

Canadians feel a thrill of pride when actress Julie Harris, in a newspaper interview, calls Christopher Plummer "the leading actor in North America," but this pride is dampened when they discover that most American readers assume that Plummer is from the U.S. Short stories by Canadian writers are listed as American in collections of American short stories. Paintings by Kenneth Lochhead, Jean-Paul Mousseau, Harold Town or Jean MacEwen would, in New York, be grouped with work done by artists of the New York School. In short, Canada has developed no school of theater, painting, literature or music which is truly distinct from work done by Americans or Europeans.

THIS is not surprising. For, until recent decades, Canadian art was largely ignored in Canada itself. Culture was considered to be the province of a few remote and inaccessible dons and the greatest barrier facing a native-born artist was the unshakable conviction of his fellow countrymen that work done by a Canadian must be inferior. This attitude was summarized by one Canadian professor thus: "The symbol of Canada is the beaver, that industrious rodent whose destiny it was to furnish hats that warmed better brains than his own." (Even today, there is an echo of this attitude in the way Canadian bookstores display all works by Canadians on a special "Canadiana" shelf—be they scenic calendars, novels, treatises on Hindu philosophy, books of poetry or sagas of the Canadian Mounted Police.)

It used to be taken as axiomatic that any Canadian who showed genuine talent in the arts would at once pack and leave for London, Paris or New York. Those who ignored this axiom did so at great cost. Their fate is summed up in the story of Frederick Philip Grove who,

THE TALLEST TOTEM POLE ever found, 81 feet high, is shown in the drawings above. On the left are side and front views of the top section of the pole; on the right are the same views of the bottom half. This pole, discovered in British Columbia in 1927 and preserved in Toronto, contains the symbols of two clans, the Eagles and the Wolves. The Indians began carving totem poles as signs of family, clan or tribal pride and prosperity in the early 19th Century.

after many unrewarding years of writing novels in and about Canada, was forced, at 71, to go out and find day labor in an Ontario canning factory. There, wrote Grove, he met another elderly man down on his luck. In conversation, he discovered that this man was a graduate of Oxford University. "How did you get here?" Grove asked. "Drink," said the man. "And you?" "Literature," replied Grove.

Grove was a man of little talent who merely had the desire to be a good writer. Yet, if he were alive today, it is likely that some Canadian official body would be sympathetic to his ambitions and his plight. For in recent years the country has undergone an astonishing change in its attitude toward art. The change began in 1949, when the federal government, worried less about Canada's lack of culture than about Canadians' ignorance of their history, set up a royal commission under the chairmanship of Vincent Massey, later governor-general. The commission was supposed to find out how Canadians could be spurred to greater "national feeling" through learning more about their history and traditions.

THE Massey commission, wisely ignoring this politicians' desire for advice on the care and feeding of nationalism, turned its attention instead to the country's cultural shortcomings. In a series of hearings it quizzed publishers, artists, teachers, musicians and other interested parties. In 1951 the commission published a report which ranks as one of the great state papers in Canada's history. Its recommendations changed Canada's cultural life, and Massey's subsequent prestige as governor-general helped to make "culture" respectable at last.

For many years Canadian governments had been lukewarm in their support for such state-financed institutions as the Canadian Broadcasting Corporation, the National Film Board, the National (Art) Gallery and the National Museum. The commission urged increased aid for these institutions, pointing out that such national identity as Canada possessed stemmed largely from their influence. But the commission's really radical proposal was for the creation of a body to be known as "The Canada Council for the Encouragement of the Arts, Letters, Humanities and Social Sciences." Surprisingly, Parliament agreed to the idea; thus, in one stroke, Canada settled a cultural question which has been debated in the United States almost since the days of the Continental Congress. By the creation of The Canada Council in 1957, the government approved the principle of state subsidy of the arts.

THE story of The Canada Council's creation illustrates, as a side issue, the amount of money which individuals can still amass in Canada. Inheritance taxes on the estates of two recently deceased multimillionaires—Sir James Dunn, a steel magnate, and I. W. Killam, a financier—had left the government with a windfall of $100 million. The Canada Council was created with this capital. The income from half of it was to be devoted to providing grants to artists and the arts. Income from the other half was to be made available to institutions of learning. As a result, the Canada Council since 1957 has become the nation's biggest impresario, and its assistance has sparked a cultural binge in every major community.

The Council helps support professional theater groups in Vancouver, Winnipeg, Toronto and Montreal. It gives grants to many of Canada's 20 symphony orchestra associations and subsidizes the two national ballet companies, the National Ballet Company of Canada and the Royal Winnipeg Ballet, as well as a third group, *Les Grands Ballets Canadiens* of Montreal. It has provided thousands of scholarships for artists, writers and students, has helped to establish a National Theater School in Montreal and has arranged for Canadian concerts by native operatic and other singers who, until recently, rarely performed in their native land. For it is a paradox in Canada that while the country boasts enough first-rank operatic singers to stock the Metropolitan in New York—including Jon Vickers, George London, Louis Quilico, Teresa Stratas, Pierrette Alarie and Leopold Simoneau—Canadians must travel to London's Covent Garden, the Metropolitan or other famous opera houses to hear them.

In the professional theater, the revival was generated not by the council but by a mild-mannered young man named Tom Patterson who, almost singlehandedly, sold Canadians on the idea of making Stratford, Ontario, a Shakespearean center that would rival that of Stratford, England. In 1953 he persuaded his fellow-townsmen in Stratford to put up enough money to hire England's Sir Tyrone Guthrie as advisor and director, and with Guthrie's enthusiastic help he built a tent theater and hired a combination of English stars and Canadian actors to do summer Shakespeare.

In the intervening years Stratford has become the foremost Shakespearean theater in North America and has broadened its scope to include such other activities as concerts, art exhibitions and a theater school. By 1956 the festival had attracted so many Canadian and American visitors that its promoters could risk using Canadian, not imported, stars. When the risk proved successful—and American newspapers were lavish in their praise of the acting—the Canadian myth of inferiority was dealt a death blow—at least in the field of the performing arts. The success of Stratford has caused a revival of professional theater in Canada. In Montreal, for instance, several French-language groups now play everything from Molière to Ionesco in professional repertory.

IN fact, with a new supply of performers, theaters and auditoriums, with a new interest in literature and with new state support for artistic endeavors, Canada is suddenly in the position of being unable to find enough first-rate native material on which it can lavish attention. Jack Ludwig, a Canadian critic, has summed up the country's present cultural dilemma by reversing the old parable of the emperor who walked naked through the streets of his capital while the people pretended he was wearing a magnificent suit of clothes. Canadian culture, says Ludwig, is now a magnificent suit of clothes which walks through the streets with no emperor inside. Canadian producers talk enthusiastically of building a Canadian theater but nervously admit that they can find no Canadian plays worth putting on. Canada has no internationally known composers, and in sculpture, ballet, opera and philosophy it has yet to develop an individual voice. Most of the genuine talent that the country has produced in writing and painting largely antedates the affluent era. The record of serious older Canadian artists makes it clear that their best work was done in conditions of almost total cultural neglect.

THUS, the Group of Seven, Canada's only national movement in painting, got started in 1920, when seven young men who worked for commercial art firms began setting out each autumn, living in a railway boxcar and painting landscapes of the Canadian wilderness in all its harsh beauty, with its strong light and spacious skies and waters, which have nothing in common with English country lanes or France's hazy, silvery air. Their canvases, which had the brilliant coloring of Fauve Post-Impressionism, changed the whole course of English Canadian painting—without, unfortunately, enriching the painters themselves. Similarly, Emily Carr, Canada's best known woman painter, lived a life of cultural isolation, her work mocked at by her philistine neighbors. Her paintings of Indian villages and totem poles now hang in many Canadian galleries, yet she lived in poverty alone with her pets.

Morley Callaghan, a friend and Paris contemporary of Ernest Hemingway and F. Scott Fitzgerald, whose short stories won him early international acclaim, might point to a similar neglect by his fellow countrymen during the 1930s, when he was doing his finest work. Callaghan, who chose to return from Paris and New York to his native Toronto, where he still lives, was for many years a neglected oddity in his native city, although he was the one serious, practicing writer Toronto possessed. The Englishman Malcolm Lowry, whose *Under the Volcano*, a remarkable novel of a drunkard's private hell in Mexico, was written in the late 1930s, worked unknown in a squatter's shack outside Vancouver. His fame in Canada came long after he had been acclaimed by leading American and European critics.

Lowry might have suffered an even longer neglect in Canada and abroad had his novel been set in a Canadian locale. Hugh MacLennan of Montreal, the only serious novelist of the 1940s whose novels later attracted a wide Canadian audience, points out that, in that period, the outside world's indifference to Canadian books added to the writers' feelings of loneliness and neglect. "A writer who wrote solely of Canadian themes knew that the lack of interest in Canada abroad would so limit his sales that he would have to take one or two extra jobs to support himself. Most of us did that."

Yet in the best work of the 1930s and 1940s, there is evidence of a special Canadian voice, a truly native accent which hints at neglect and despair, which evokes the huge and frightening landscape of the country. This voice is clearly discernible in the best Canadian poetry of this period and in work as diverse as Callaghan's fine short stories, the raw landscapes of the Group of Seven and Gabrielle Roy's portrait of the pinched lives of the French urban poor. It remains to be seen if, in an age when young Canadian artists receive fellowship assistance more easily than their English, American or French counterparts, this voice will die.

IN the meantime, other countries might profit by keeping an eye on Canada's experiment of culture by fiat. It is still too soon to say if, by wanting it and paying for it, a nation can develop its own voice in the arts. Canada's artistic achievements are, to date, mainly a reflection of styles formed elsewhere. But it must be remembered that, until an American voice emerged 100 years ago in the works of Walt Whitman and Herman Melville, the same could have been said of the United States. For if culture follows nationhood as crops follow seeds, then Canada has only begun to sow.

A LEADING ACTRESS of Canada, Kate Reid, who has also had brilliant successes in England and the U.S., discusses a part with Michael Langham, a director at Canada's Stratford Shakespearean Festival.

The Arts Triumphing Over Long Neglect

Canadian artists long suffered neglect at the hands of their countrymen. One source of this neglect was the unfortunate, though understandable, philistinism of a new country which naturally paid homage to builders and doers—the vivid and vigorous men who were taming the land. Another source was a curious self-distrust which prevented Canadians from accepting their native artists until they had gained fame in London, Paris or New York. But a number of painters and writers of considerable power persevered, and in recent years the cultural climate has changed. Theater, ballet and opera companies have been born, the older artists rediscovered and young men encouraged to create a new and vigorous Canadian art.

PROBING CREATORS are at work in literature, science and motion pictures

COMMUNICATIONS EXPERT Marshall McLuhan, a former University of Toronto professor now teaching in the U.S., has provoked controversy with books like *Understanding Media*.

WORLD-FAMOUS SURGEON, Dr. Wilder Penfield *(opposite),* born in the U.S., has taught and practiced neurosurgery in Canada since 1928. He became a Canadian citizen in 1934.

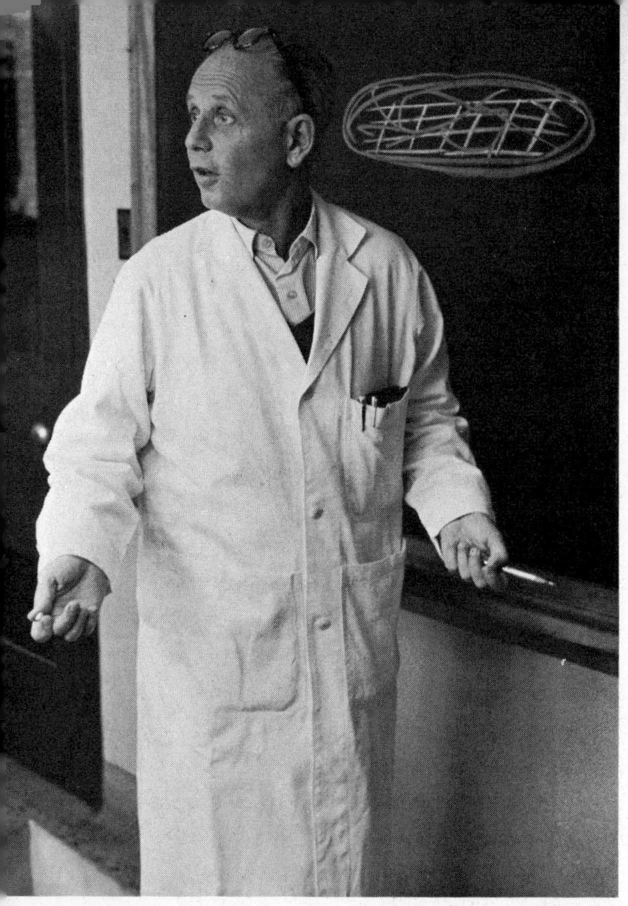

BRILLIANT THEORIST on the role of nervous stress in causing disease, Dr. Hans Selye, an Austrian immigrant, heads Montreal's Institute of Experimental Medicine and Surgery.

INVENTIVE FILM MAKER, Norman McLaren makes a fine art of the animated cartoon by painting vivid abstract shapes on film and wittily joining them with musical sound tracks.

PERCEPTIVE NOVELIST, Hugh MacLennan examines Canadian society in his fiction. *Two Solitudes* (1945), considered by many to be his best novel, deals with French-English tension.

VERSATILE CRAFTSMAN, Harold Town stands before a rack of finished oil paintings in his Toronto studio. Town also works in collage and graphic arts and is a recognized sculptor.

COLOR EXPERIMENTALIST, Yves Gaucher of Montreal, shown with his wife, turns out monochromatic canvases whose colors, said one critic, "imprint themselves on the very soul."

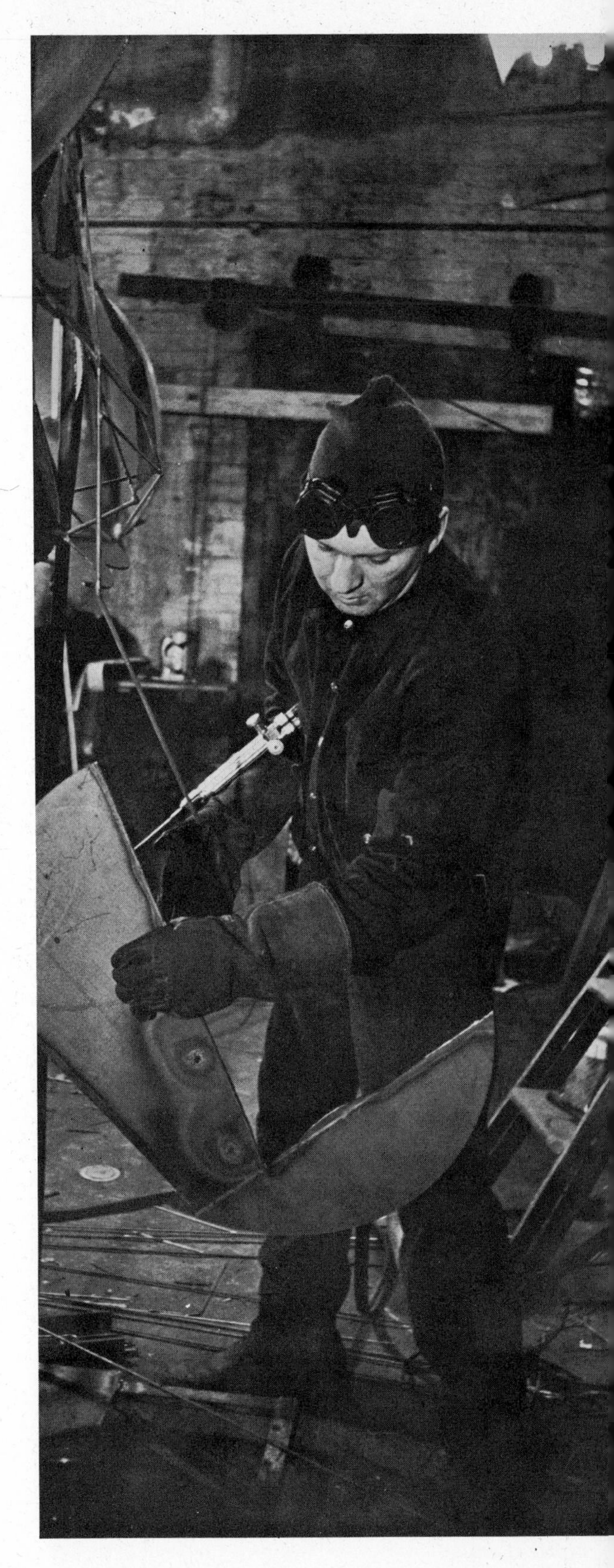

AVANT-GARDE SCULPTOR, Gerald Gladstone works on a metal construction in his studio. Like many other young Canadian artists, Gladstone was helped by a government grant.

YOUNG ARTISTS work at home but continue the bold experiments of their expatriate predecessors

BRILLIANT COLORS characteristic of the work of Jean-Paul Riopelle are clearly evident in *La Roue, No. 2 (right)*. Born in French Canada, Riopelle has lived in Paris since 1945 and has now won an international reputation.

LUMINOUS CANVAS by the late Paul-Emile Borduas shows a step in his development from a landscape painter into a master of abstract composition. A native of Quebec, Borduas worked in both New York and Paris.

LANDSCAPES of rugged countryside entranced earlier artists, some of whom formed the "Group of Seven"

ONTARIO LAKE shimmers with color *(left)* in a 1915 canvas by Tom Thomson, whose work was influenced by Impressionism. Thomson foreshadowd the Group of Seven, but he died too early to belong.

ALBERTA WHEATFIELD epitomizes autumn in a bold painting by A. Y. Jackson. Jackson was one of the Group of Seven who took painting trips together in the 1920s to record the look of Canada's wilds.

INDIAN STATUES gaze at the water in *Blunden Harbour,* a starkly simple canvas by Emily Carr. A British Columbia native, Miss Carr devoted her life to painting the people and countryside of the West Coast.

NORTHERN UPLAND is characteristic of the strong paintings *(opposite)* of J.E.H. MacDonald, who borrowed some of the swirling forms of Van Gogh to capture the grandeur of the Canadian wilderness.

QUEBEC SCHOOLBOYS eat their lunchtime sandwiches on the sunny promenade of Dufferin Terrace, a handsome boardwalk, opened in 1838, that commands a magnificent panorama of the St. Lawrence River and Quebec's famous Old Town.

10

Dilemmas and Promises

THE year 1967 occasioned historic celebrations in the two largest countries on earth. In Russia, it marked the 50th anniversary of the Revolution, an event which transformed a huge, backward, feudal country into one of the most powerful nations in history. In Canada, it marked the 100th anniversary of the act of Confederation, which united a huge, backward, colonial country into a nation.

There is a curious irony in the results of these events. The Russian Revolution was an attempt to set up an international Communist movement in which national differences would wither away. The Canadian Confederation was an attempt to set up a separate nation which would resist the threat of American expansionist tendencies. Half a century later, Russia is more nationalist than ever and national rivalries weaken the Communist empire. One hundred years later, Canada remains unsure of its national character and most national differences between Canadians and Americans have withered away.

The Russian celebrations were observed in Moscow's Red Square with an awesome display of tanks, troops and nuclear missiles. The festivities in Canada were more peaceful, but no less impressive. They began on New Year's Eve, when a Centennial flame was lit on top of

Ottawa's Parliament Hill, and they continued throughout the year with a potpourri of local celebrations and cultural events. A special exhibition train toured the nation, and a Youth Travel Program sent thousands of teenagers on cross-country trips outside their own province.

But the star of the Centennial birthday party was Montreal's Expo 67. A cooperative effort by the federal government, Canada's provinces, the city of Montreal, Expo was an exciting and highly successful blend of Anglo-Saxon competence and French Canadian verve. It attracted 50 million visitors from all over the globe, decreased Canada's balance-of-payments deficit by $500 million, and demonstrated to the world at large—and most importantly, to the Canadians themselves—a new sense of national identity and self-esteem.

DESPITE Expo, however, Canadians still see their difficulties almost completely in terms of national identity. They can no longer find a satisfactory self-image in their old associations with Great Britain. Since World War II, they have watched their export market in Britain almost cut in half. In the same period the country has witnessed the decline of the present-day Commonwealth to an honorary association of divergent peoples. While the old ties to Britain have decayed, Canada has come increasingly under the economic aegis of the United States, and many Canadians now fear that theirs is merely a branch-plant economy of their neighbor to the south. In addition, the country, as never before, is divided by antagonism between Quebec and the rest of Canada.

Under these circumstances, it is not surprising that the search for a strong and shared sense of nationality should be at the forefront of Canadian concerns. It is, to Canadians, a relatively new search and no one can predict its future direction.

At the time of Confederation, a majority of Canadians knew who they were: they were British, French, Yankee or European settlers, and their attitude to Canada and the United States was summed up by a Scottish immigrant farmer who was asked on which side of the border his land lay. "I don't know," he said. "It's a' America tae me."

This idea that it's "a' America" not only economically but also culturally now disturbs Canadians, as it has older and more settled nations with, it would seem, a very firm sense of their identities. In this "American age," even countries such as Britain and France have begun to worry about the Americanization of their people. If such a thing can happen there, Canadians ask, what chance have we of avoiding our much greater risk of contagion?

Yet the comparison is inexact. The Americanization of Western European nations stems from a rise in the postwar standard of living and a more democratic set of working conditions. Canada has long had this higher standard of living, and even before World War II its population had adopted American working conditions. Therefore this process of Americanization, or democratization, which is relatively new to France and Britain, is an old story to Canadians and it seems unlikely that further exposure to American ways can make any far-reaching alterations in Canadian habits of life. Nor will a new Canadian identity be found through attempts to de-Americanize the Canadian people. Achievement of this identity will depend not on pro- or anti-American stances, but on raising the standard of national taste, on promoting cultural excellence and on inculcating in the average Canadian a respect for achievement in the arts, sciences, government and humanities that equals his present respect for those who accumulate great wealth.

IN the early 1960s, the question of nuclear weapons and North American defense was used by politicians anxious to exploit Canadian fears of outside influence and big-power domination. Many Canadians believed that if their government accepted nuclear warheads for Canadian missiles and operated joint defense installations with the United States, a Russian nuclear holocaust would descend on Canadian cities. Yet the record shows a decreasing (rather than increasing) American influence on Canada's defense policies. Since 1954, when the Canadian government spent 42.7 per cent of the national budget on defense, later governments voted budgets in which this percentage dropped until, in 1966, it fell to 20 per cent. This hardly seems the course which a slavish satellite of the United States would adopt.

BY 1968, Canada seemed ready to make some changes in its defense posture. It had already sided with France and against the United States on the removal of NATO headquarters from Paris. The country's new prime minister, Pierre Elliott Trudeau, before taking office in April 1968, made a casually worded declaration of independence in the general area of defense and foreign policy. "We should not be guided so uniquely by what our friends in Washington and London think," he said.

In other areas, it seemed as if Trudeau were about to impart a new look to Canadian affairs. A former law professor from the University of Montreal, he became prime minister at age 48 after only three years in active politics, first as a Liberal party representative from Quebec, and then as justice minister in the Cabinet of Lester Pearson. As a hard-working cabinet member he had initiated a number of important legal reforms. To voters, he projected an image of breezy nonconformity, wearing sandals and an ascot and driving a sports car. In a short time he came to symbolize the desire for change in Canada, and when Pearson announced his retirement, Trudeau was elected to replace him in a sudden wave of popular support.

Much of Trudeau's popularity came from his work as architect of the Liberal party's constitutional policy. One of Pearson's last official acts was to call together representatives from each of the provinces to reassess their relationship with the federal government, and in effect to draw up a new constitution. With the centrifugal pull of the Separatist forces in Quebec, a successful outcome would mean, according to Pearson, "no less than Canada's survival as a nation." Under the Trudeau plan, the new constitution would include a Bill of Rights for all Canadians, establish both English and French as official languages, and "make equality of economic and cultural opportunity as real and meaningful for Canadians of French origins as it is for English-speaking Canadians." Though Trudeau is a French Canadian, he is also a federalist, and as prime minister he was expected to redouble the Liberal party effort to weld together the Canadian Confederation.

In economics, Trudeau took a moderate stand on the issue of United States investment in Canadian business. With American investors now owning or controlling more than half of Canadian manufacturing capacity and an ever-larger share of the petroleum and natural gas industry, it seems unavoidable that Canadians must place their economic hopes on even closer business ties with the U.S. Instead of fighting this trend, Trudeau would seek to bring the freewheeling American interests under tighter control by Canadian law, and at the same time encourage participation in key sectors by Canadians themselves. Canada must begin, Trudeau said, by "investing in the future, not buying back the past." Possible moves would be to continue the Liberal policies of greater trade with Latin America and the Communist countries, and the setting up of programs already suggested by Liberal economists for encouraging investment in domestic industries.

THE most highly touted of these plans would be to float a Canadian Development Corporation which would lend money to Canadian enterprises at favorable terms and temporarily buy up controlling interest in essential industries that are in danger of being devoured by foreign investors. The Canadian public would support this Corporation by buying shares, just as they bought government bonds during the war. The weakness in this proposition is the proven past record of the Canadian public. Canadians will not count patriotism as one extra interest point in making a financial investment.

But, if fears of U.S. domination over their

industries continue to haunt Canadian politicians, there is a consolation in knowing that the U.S. stake in Canada will help provide the capital and the technical know-how needed to ensure healthy economic growth. More American money—an estimated $27.5 billion by 1967—has been invested in Canada than in any single other foreign country, a proof that Americans continue to believe that Canada is economically sound and will remain so.

VIEWED hopefully, therefore, the alliance between Canada and America may become one of interdependence. For Canada is a small nation only in the size of its population and in the present stage of its development. Potentially it remains "the Russia of the New World." But Canadians cannot develop it with their limited resources of men, money and technical skills. Again, America would seem the logical partner to share in the work and to benefit from the future development of Canada's far north. For Canada is now, irrevocably, a North American nation committed to a North American future, and its great unconquered land area is the last North American frontier. Only in Canada can future generations find the "New West" that they will eventually need for the continent's growth.

In the past, Canadians have feared closer economic ties with the United States because these ties might tend to bind Canada politically to the U.S. This fear of closeness has been based on a Canadian belief that two different systems of government prevailed in Canada and in the U.S. But, as the historian F. H. Underhill recently pointed out, "our [Canadian] political parties called themselves by British names and worked within a framework of British parliamentary democracy, but the politics they practiced were American."

Professor Underhill says that this Americanization dates back to the days of Confederation itself, when, to build the railway that would make union possible, Canada's government gave money grants, land grants and monopoly privileges to the privately run Canadian Pacific Railway. That action inaugurated "an alliance between government and big business which has become the characteristic feature of . . . Canadian politics."

This, he emphasizes, is "an American kind of politics," a kind of politics in which a business mentality influences public policies. Because of this, according to Underhill, Canada and the United States are ideologically closer to each other than either country is to Britain or France.

Certainly, in the past, this feeling that politics were influenced by big business interests and were therefore "dull" contributed to the apathy with which most educated Canadians regarded the political scene. This is no longer true. Unlike America, Canada is not a world power, and future Canadian governments will not be forced into the essentially conservative postures which a leader of the Western alliance must maintain. In this respect Canada is like a younger brother, freed of much responsibility and susceptible to experiment. There is abroad in the country today a feeling comparable to that of a younger America, a feeling that parties and institutions are not securely entrenched, a feeling that the electorate can still "kick the rascals out."

THIS notion that anything is possible has resulted in a new unrest, especially among the younger generation which is no longer content with that "sense of limitations" to which their parents so proudly confessed. An alarm light seems to have lit up the country: Canadians feel that anything may happen. Quebec could secede, Canada could disarm, it could join the U.S. If none of these things seems probable, they are all possible and contribute to the heady uncertainty which has gripped Canadians. Abbé O'Neill, a Quebec churchman, spoke of French Canada in words which seem to apply to the nation as a whole. It is, he said, "like a man in a canoe, going over a set of rapids. He can steer—he must steer, or he will crash on a rock—but he cannot get out and he cannot turn around."

Arches span a reflecting pool before Toronto's new City Hall. Next page: Snow-capped peaks rise on the Yukon-Alaska border.

A DETERMINED EFFORT *which has established a great industrial nation . . .*

. . . must be renewed and revitalized if Canada, with its boundless natural resources,

is fully to realize its tremendous potential for growth and prosperity and power.

Appendix

HISTORICAL DATES

A.D.

- c.1000 Vikings are believed to have reached the Canadian coast
- 1497 John Cabot, in the British service, discovers the North American coast. Britain subsequently lays claim to Newfoundland and Nova Scotia
- 1534-1541 Jacques Cartier explores the St. Lawrence Gulf and River for France. His attempts to plant a colony fail
- 1605 Samuel de Champlain and his patron, the Sieur de Monts, found the Acadian settlement of Port Royal
- 1608 Champlain founds the city of Quebec. He enlists aid from several Indian tribes to support the expanding fur trade but alienates the Iroquois
- 1610-1611 Henry Hudson, commissioned by Britain to find the Northwest Passage, discovers and explores Hudson Bay
- 1627 Louis XIII of France grants a trade monopoly to the Company of One Hundred Associates, with authority to colonize and govern New France
- 1642 The Sieur de Maisonneuve heads a French mission which founds Montreal
- 1648-1660 The Iroquois increasingly harass the French and their Indian allies. United finally, and armed by Dutch traders, they threaten New France with extinction
- 1663 Louis XIV cancels the charter of the One Hundred Associates and rules New France directly
- 1670 Investors in England headed by Prince Rupert organize Hudson's Bay Company. By fur trading out of the bay it avoids the French routes
- 1689-1763 French and Indian Wars. Contest for control of the continent brings French and British colonists into armed conflict, complicated by their Indian alliances and by European wars
- 1713 France cedes Acadia to Britain and gives up its claim to Hudson Bay and Newfoundland
- 1731-1744 La Vérendrye sets up fur-trading posts as he explores westward to the Saskatchewan River
- 1749-1755 The British colonize Nova Scotia. Doubting the loyalty of the Acadian French, the British expel and scatter them along the Atlantic coast
- 1759 Quebec falls to the British. Both Wolfe and Montcalm, British and French generals, die in the battle
- 1760 British capture Montreal
- 1763 In the wake of losses both in America and Europe, France cedes its North American territories east of the Mississippi to Britain
- 1774 By the Quebec Act Britain enlarges the boundaries of Quebec province, confirms freedom of religion for Catholics and imposes a combination of British and French law
- 1775-1783 During the American Revolution, American colonists who remain loyal to Britain during the war flee across the Canadian border. American attacks on Quebec fail
- 1776-1793 Explorations by Captains James Cook and George Vancouver open the Pacific Northwest coast to trade. Alexander Mackenzie completes a long cross-country expedition
- 1783-1787 Montreal merchants form the North West Company in order to compete more effectively with the Hudson's Bay Company
- 1791 Quebec is divided into Upper and Lower Canada, each with an elected assembly. Emigrants from the U.S. by now make up a substantial part of Upper Canada's population
- 1812-1814 War of 1812 between the U.S. and Britain. U.S. forces invade the Canadas but make no gains. The peace treaty provides for U.S.-Canadian boundary settlements
- 1821 North West and Hudson's Bay Companies merge
- 1837-1838 Separate rebellions growing out of political reform attempts are led by Louis-Joseph Papineau in Lower Canada and William Lyon Mackenzie in Upper Canada. Both are put down swiftly
- 1838 The Earl of Durham, sent from England to recommend reforms, urges union for the Canadas and a system of responsible government
- 1842-1846 Treaties fix the New Brunswick-Maine and Oregon Territory boundaries
- 1847-1854 Governorship of the Earl of Elgin, under whom responsible government is instituted in Canada despite a period of political and economic crisis. A reciprocity treaty is negotiated with the U.S.
- 1858 Gold rush to the Fraser River
- 1864 Agreement for Confederation is reached at conferences in Charlottetown and Quebec
- 1867 British North America Act unites the provinces of the Canadas (divided into Ontario and Quebec), Nova Scotia and New Brunswick as the Dominion of Canada, with its capital at Ottawa. Conservative John A. Macdonald is the first prime minister
- 1869 The vast landholdings of Hudson's Bay Company are transferred to Canada
- 1869-1885 Louis Riel leads two uprisings, primarily involving *metis* (half-breeds) and Indians in the midwestern territories. Riel is captured and executed for treason
- 1873 North West Mounted Police are organized
- 1881-1885 The Canadian Pacific Railway is built
- 1896 Wilfrid Laurier, Liberal, becomes the first French Canadian prime minister. Gold is discovered in the Klondike
- 1903 Alaskan boundary is settled
- 1914-1918 Canadian participation in World War I. Passage of the Conscription Bill deepens antagonisms between French and English Canadians
- 1921 William Lyon Mackenzie King, Liberal, becomes prime minister and dominates Canadian politics for three decades
- 1931 Canada gains complete self-rule by the Statute of Westminster
- 1930-1940 Depression in Canada, paralleling that in U.S., gives rise to Cooperative Commonwealth Federation and Social Credit parties in the Prairies
- 1939-1945 Canadian participation in World War II
- 1945 Canada joins the United Nations and takes an increasingly important role in world affairs
- 1949 Canada joins the North Atlantic Treaty Organization
- 1954 Construction is begun on U.S.-Canadian joint defense warning systems
- 1957 Conservatives, with John Diefenbaker as prime minister, take over the government
- 1959 St. Lawrence Seaway opened
- 1963 Liberals regain power with Lester B. Pearson as prime minister
- 1968 Pierre Elliott Trudeau becomes prime minister after Lester Pearson's resignation

FOR FURTHER READING

CHAPTER 1: THE LAND AND ITS PEOPLE

Brebner, J. B., *Canada*. University of Michigan Press, 1960.

Brown, George W., ed., *Canada*. University of California Press, 1950.

Canada 1867-1967. Dominion Bureau of Statistics. Ottawa, 1967.

Careless, James M. S., *Canada; A Story of Challenge*. Cambridge University Press, 1953.

Hannon, Leslie F., ed., *Maclean's Canada: Portrait of a Country*. McClelland & Stewart, Toronto, 1960.

Hutchison, Bruce, *The Unknown Country*. Longmans, Green, Toronto, 1948.

Lang, Gladys E., ed., *Canada*. H. W. Wilson, 1959.

Massey, Vincent, *Canadians and Their Commonwealth*. Oxford University Press, 1961.

Masters, Donald C., *A Short History of Canada*. Anvil Original, 1958.

McInnis, Edgar, *Canada*. Holt, Rinehart and Winston, 1959.

Siegfried, André, *Canada, An International Power*. Duell, Sloan & Pearce, 1959.

CHAPTER 2: HISTORY (GENERAL)

Allen, Ralph, *Ordeal By Fire; Canada, 1910-1945*. Doubleday, 1961.

Brown, George W., *Canada in the Making*. University of Washington Press, 1953.

Costain, Thomas B., *The White and the Gold*. Doubleday, 1954.

Creighton, Donald, *The Story of Canada*. Houghton Mifflin, 1960. *History of Canada: Dominion of the North*. 1958. *The Empire of the St. Lawrence*. 1958.

Hardy, William G., *From Sea Unto Sea*. Doubleday, 1960.

Howard, Joseph Kinsey, *Strange Empire: A Narrative of the Northwest*. William Morrow, 1952.

Kidd, Kenneth E., *Canadians of Long Ago*. Longmans, Green, Toronto, 1959.

Lower, Arthur R. M., *Colony to Nation*. Longmans Canada, Toronto, 1961.

MacLennan, Hugh, *The Rivers of Canada*. Charles Scribner's Sons, 1961.

Mahoney, Tom, *The Great Merchants*. Harper & Brothers, 1955.

Martin, Chester B., *Foundations of Canadian Nationhood*. University of Toronto Press, 1955.

McKay, Douglas, *The Honourable Company*. Bobbs-Merrill, 1936.

Parkman, Francis, *The Parkman Reader*. Samuel Eliot Morison, ed., Little, Brown, 1955.

Priestley, Herbert I., *History of American Life*, Vol. 1, *The Coming of the White Man, 1492-1848*. Macmillan, 1929.

Wrong, George M., *Canada and the American Revolution*. Macmillan, 1935.

CHAPTER 3: ECONOMICS AND POLITICS

Easterbrook, William T., and Hugh G. J. Aitken, *Canadian Economic History*. Macmillan of Canada, Toronto, 1958.

Fox, Paul, ed., *Politics: Canada*. McGraw-Hill of Canada, Toronto, 1962.

Gordon, Walter L., *Troubled Canada*. McClelland & Stewart, Toronto, 1961.

Innis, Harold A., *Essays in Canadian Economic History*. University of Toronto Press, 1956.

CHAPTER 4: THE NATIONAL IDENTITY

Barber, Joseph, *Good Fences Make Good Neighbors*. McClelland & Stewart, Toronto, 1958.

Falardeau, Jean-C., *Roots and Values in Canadian Lives*. University of Toronto Press, 1961.

Horne, Alistair, *Canada and the Canadians*. Macmillan of Canada, Toronto, 1961.

Massey, Vincent, *On Being Canadian*. J. M. Dent & Sons, Toronto, 1948.

Morton, William L., *The Canadian Identity*. University of Wisconsin Press, 1961.

Russell, Peter, editor, *Nationalism in Canada*. McGraw-Hill, 1966.

Wrong, Dennis H., *American and Canadian Viewpoints*. American Council on Education, 1956.

CHAPTER 5: CANADA'S SOCIAL STRUCTURE

Blishen, Bernard R., ed., and others, *Canadian Society*. Macmillan of Canada, Toronto, 1961.

Clark, Samuel, D., *The Social Development of Canada*. University of Toronto Press, 1946.

Lower, Arthur R. M., *Canadians in the Making*. Longmans, Green, Toronto, 1958.

McInnis, Edgar W., *Canada, A Political and Social History*. Holt, Rinehart & Winston of Canada, Toronto, 1959.

Underhill, Frank H., *In Search of Canadian Liberalism*. St. Martins Press, 1960.

Vickers, Geoffrey, *Undirected Society*. University of Toronto Press, 1959.

CHAPTER 6: CHANGE IN QUEBEC

Chapin, Miriam, *Quebec Now*. Oxford University Press, 1955.

Hughes, Everett C., *French Canada in Transition*. University of Chicago Press, 1943.

Wade, Mason, *The French Canadians, 1760-1945*. Macmillan of Canada, Toronto, 1955. *The French-Canadian Outlook*. Viking Press, 1946.

CHAPTER 7: THE EMPTY NORTH

Berton, Pierre, *The Mysterious North*. Alfred A. Knopf, 1956.

Calder, Peter Ritchie, *Men Against the Frozen North*. Macmillan, 1957.

Cooper, Paul Fenimore, *Island of the Lost*. G. P. Putnam's Sons, 1961.

Freuchen, Peter and Finn Salomonsen, *The Arctic Year*. G. P. Putnam's Sons, 1958.

Mowat, Farley, ed., *Ordeal By Ice*. Little, Brown, 1961.

Olson, Sigurd F., *The Lonely Land*. Alfred A. Knopf, 1961.

CHAPTER 8: WAVES OF IMMIGRATION

Bouscaren, Anthony T., *International Migrations Since 1945*. Frederick A. Praeger, 1963.

Corbett, David C., *Canada's Immigration Policy*. University of Toronto Press, Toronto, 1957.

Cowan, Helen I., *British Emigration to British North America, The First Hundred Years*. University of Toronto Press, 1961.

Timlin, Mabel F., *Does Canada Need More People?* Oxford University Press, Toronto, 1951.

CHAPTER 9: LITERATURE AND ART

Buchanan, Donald W., *The Growth of Canadian Painting*. William Collins Sons, Toronto, 1950.

McInnes, Graham, *Canadian Art*. Macmillan of Canada, Toronto, 1950.

Park, Julian, ed., *The Culture of Contemporary Canada*. Cornell University Press, 1957.

Report for the Royal Commission in the Arts, Letters and Sciences, 1949-1951. Edmund Cloutier, Ottawa, 1951.

Ross, Malcolm, ed., *The Arts in Canada*. Macmillan of Canada, Toronto, 1959.

Smith, A.J.M., ed., *A Book of Canadian Poetry*. University of Chicago Press, 1943.

Weaver, Robert, ed., *The First Five Years*. Oxford University Press, 1962.

CHAPTER 10: DILEMMAS AND PROMISES

Chapin, Miriam, *Contemporary Canada*. Oxford University Press, 1959.

Clarkson, Stephen, editor, *An Independent Foreign Policy for Canada?* McClelland and Stewart, Toronto/Montreal, 1968.

Gilmour, G. P., ed., *Canada's Tomorrow*. St. Martins Press, 1962.

Hutchison, Bruce, *Canada, Tomorrow's Giant*. Alfred A. Knopf, 1961.

FAMOUS CANADIAN CULTURAL FIGURES AND THEIR PRINCIPAL WORKS

Architecture and Sculpture

Name	Dates	Principal Works
Levasseur, Noël	1680-1740	Sculpture: wood retable in Quebec's Ursuline Chapel
Baillairgé, François	1759-1830	Sculpture: wood carvings, primarily for the church
Hébert, Louis-Philippe	1850-1917	Sculpture: classical bronze statuary for Quebec Parliament
Allward, Walter	1876-1955	*Art nouveau* sculpture. Vimy Ridge Memorial in France
Wood, Elizabeth	1903-1966	Sculpture: landscape abstractions such as *Reef and Rainbow, Passing Rain*
Archambault, Louis	1915-	Sculpture: ceramic wall for the Canadian Pavilion at the Brussels World Fair
Thom, Ronald	1923-	Architecture: Massey College in Toronto
Parkin, John	1922-	Architecture: International Airport in Toronto
Dickinson, Peter	1925-1961	Architecture: Montreal's Canadian Imperial Bank of Commerce
Grossman, Irving	1926-	Architecture: residential developments for which he effectively blends land and buildings
Gladstone, Gerald	1929-	Welded metal "space" sculptures
Vaillancourt, Armand	1932-	Sculpture: welded metal and burnt wood abstractions

Painting

Name	Dates	Principal Works
Plamondon, Antoine	1804-1895	Portraits and religious works for churches, combining classic line and limpid colors
Kane, Paul	1810-1871	Series of portraits and scenes from Indian life, of considerable historic interest
Krieghoff, Cornelius	1815-1872	Scenes from habitant and Indian life, landscapes and portraits. Canada's "old master"
Hamel, Theophile	1817-1870	Gentle, contemplative portraits in the romantic manner
Morrice, James Wilson	1865-1924	Soft-colored, melancholy oils. Post-Impressionist pioneer; a student and friend of Matisse
Suzor-Coté, Aurèle de Foy	1869-1937	Impressionistic figures and landscapes of French Canadian subjects. Also a sculptor
Carr, Emily	1871-1945	Powerfully expressive oils and watercolors of Indians and landscapes of British Columbia
MacDonald, James Edward Hervey	1873-1932	Landscapes. Founder of the Group of Seven
Thomson, Tom	1877-1917	Landscapes. Inspirational force, although not a member, of the Group of Seven
Varley, Frederick Horsman	1881-	Landscapes and portraits. Member of the Group of Seven
Milne, David	1882-1953	Sensitive, highly personal landscapes, fantasies and still life in water color and oil
Jackson, Alexander Young	1882-	Landscapes. Member of the Group of Seven
Harris, Lawren	1885-	Keystone of the Group of Seven. Painted landscapes until turning to abstractions
Lismer, Arthur	1885-	Landscapes. Member of the Group of Seven; works with children in art education
Macdonald, Jock	1897-1957	Abstractions. Founder of Painters Eleven
Lemieux, Jean-Paul	1904-	Solitary figure studies in oil
Borduas, Paul-Emile	1905-1960	Pioneer of abstract art. Founder and leader of the *automatiste* group in Montreal
Wilson, Ronald York	1907-	Abstract oils and murals
Riopelle, Jean-Paul	1923-	*Tachist* oils, with superb coloring
Town, Harold	1924-	"Autographic" prints, oils, etchings, collages
Gaucher, Yves	1934-	Embossed white prints, monochromatic paintings

Literature

Name	Dates	Principal Works
Gaspé, Philippe Aubert de	1786-1871	Novel: *Les Anciens Canadiens*
Haliburton, Thomas Chandler	1796-1865	Sam Slick stories: *The Clockmaker*
Garneau, François-Xavier	1809-1866	History: *Histoire du Canada*
Crémazie, Octave	1827-1879	Poetry: *Le Drapeau de Carillon, Le Canada*
Connor, Ralph (Charles W. Gordon)	1860-1937	Popular romantic novels: *The Man from Glengarry*
Roberts, Charles G. D.	1860-1943	Poetry: *Orion, Songs of the Common Day*. Animal stories
Lampman, Archibald	1861-1899	Poetry: *Among the Millet, Lyrics of Earth*
Scott, Duncan Campbell	1862-1947	Poetry: *The Magic House, The Forsaken*
Leacock, Stephen Butler	1869-1944	Humorous essays and stories: *Sunshine Sketches of a Little Town, Behind the Beyond*
Service, Robert William	1874-1958	Yukon ballads and stories: *The Spell of the Yukon*
Nelligan, Emile	1879-1941	Poetry: *Poésie complète*
Pratt, Edwin John	1883-1964	Poetry: *The Roosevelt and the Antinoe, The Titanic, Brébeuf and His Brethren*
De La Roche, Mazo	1885-1961	Novels: *Jalna* and numerous other Whiteoak family sagas
Morin, Paul	1889-1963	Poetry: *Le Paon d'émail, Poèmes de cendre et d'or*
Wilson, Ethel	1890-	Novels: *Swamp Angel, Love and Salt Water*
Ringuet (Philippe Panneton)	1895-1960	Novel: *Thirty Acres*
Callaghan, Morley	1903-	Novels: *They Shall Inherit the Earth, The Loved and the Lost*
MacLennan, Hugh	1907-	Novel: *Two Solitudes*
Roy, Gabrielle	1909-	Novels: *The Tin Flute, Alexandre Chênevert*
Klein, Abraham	1909-	Poetry: *The Rocking Chair*
Garneau, St. Denys	1912-1943	Poetry: *Regards et jeux dans l'espace*. Journals
Frye, Northrop	1912-	Literary criticism: *Anatomy of Criticism*
Layton, Irving	1912-	Poetry: *The Improved Binoculars, In the Midst of My Fever*
Elie, Robert	1915-	Novel: *Farewell My Dreams*
Hébert, Anne	1916-	Poetry: *Le Tombeau des rois*. Poetic stories: *Le Torrent*
Reaney, James	1926-	Poetry: *The Red Heart*
Langevin, André	1927-	Novel: *Dust over the City*
Dubé, Marcel	1930-	Plays: *Zone, Florence, Un Simple Soldat*
Richler, Mordecai	1931-	Novel: *Son of a Smaller Hero*
Blais, Marie-Claire	1939-	Novel: *A Season in the Life of Emmanuel*

PRIME MINISTERS SINCE 1867

1. Sir John A. Macdonald (Conservative) 1867-1873
2. Alexander Mackenzie (Liberal) 1873-1878
3. Sir John A. Macdonald (Conservative) 1878-1891
4. Sir John J. C. Abbott (Conservative) 1891-1892
5. Sir John S. D. Thompson (Conservative) 1892-1894
6. Sir Mackenzie Bowell (Conservative) 1894-1896
7. Sir Charles Tupper (Conservative) 1896
8. Sir Wilfrid Laurier (Liberal) 1896-1911
9. Sir Robert L. Borden (Conservative) 1911-1917
10. Sir Robert L. Borden (Conservative: Unionist Administration) 1917-1920
11. Arthur Meighen (Conservative: Unionist Administration) 1920-1921
12. William Lyon Mackenzie King (Liberal) 1921-1926
13. Arthur Meighen (Conservative) 1926
14. William Lyon Mackenzie King (Liberal) 1926-1930
15. Richard Bedford Bennett (Conservative) 1930-1935
16. William Lyon Mackenzie King (Liberal) 1935-1948
17. Louis Stephen St. Laurent (Liberal) 1948-1957
18. John G. Diefenbaker (Progressive Conservative) 1957-1963
19. Lester B. Pearson (Liberal) 1963-1968
20. Pierre Elliott Trudeau (Liberal) 1968-

GOVERNORS-GENERAL SINCE 1867

1. Charles Stanley Monck, 4th Viscount Monck 1867-1868
2. John Young, 1st Baron Lisgar of Lisgar 1869-1872
3. Frederick Temple Hamilton-Temple Blackwood, Earl of Dufferin and Viscount Clandeboye 1872-1878
4. John Douglas Sutherland Campbell, 9th Marquess of Kintyre and Lorne 1878-1883
5. Henry Charles Keith Petty-Fitzmaurice, 5th Marquess of Lansdowne 1883-1888
6. Frederick Arthur Stanley, 1st Baron Stanley 1888-1893
7. John Campbell Gordon, 7th Earl and 1st Marquess of Aberdeen and Temair 1893-1898
8. Gilbert John Murray-Kynnynmond Elliot, 4th Earl of Minto 1898-1904
9. Albert Henry George Grey, 4th Earl Grey 1904-1911
10. Arthur William Patrick Albert, Field Marshal H.R.H. the 1st Duke of Connaught and Strathearn 1911-1916
11. Victor Christian William Cavendish, 9th Duke of Devonshire 1916-1921
12. General Julian Hedworth George Byng, Baron Byng of Vimy 1921-1926
13. Freeman Freeman-Thomas, 1st Viscount Willingdon 1926-1931
14. Vere Brabazon Ponsonby, 9th Earl of Bessborough 1931-1935
15. John Buchan, 1st Baron Tweedsmuir 1935-1940
16. Maj. Gen. Albert George Cambridge, Earl of Athlone 1940-1946
17. Field Marshal Sir Rupert Leofric George Alexander, 1st Viscount Alexander of Tunis 1946-1952
18. Rt. Hon. Vincent Massey 1952-1959
19. Gen. the Rt. Hon. Georges Philias Vanier 1959-1967
20. Rt. Hon. Roland Michener 1967-

FACTS ABOUT CANADA

NAME	CAPITAL	POP.	AREA (sq. mi.)	CONFEDERATION DATE	RESOURCES AND INDUSTRIES
Canada	**Ottawa**	**20,015,000**	**3,851,809**	**1867**	**Pulp and paper, smelting-refining, cattle, dairy products, wheat, oil, nickel**
Alberta	Edmonton	1,463,000	255,285	1905	Meat packing, oil, wheat, cattle, natural gas, hogs
British Columbia	Victoria	1,874,000	366,255	1871	Lumber, pulp and paper, dairy products, cattle, fruit, zinc, lead
Manitoba	Winnipeg	963,000	251,000	1870	Meat packing, wheat, cattle, dairy products, hogs, nickel, oil
New Brunswick	Fredericton	617,000	28,354	1867	Pulp and paper, lumber, fish, potatoes
Newfoundland	St. John's	492,000	156,185	1949	Pulp and paper, fish, iron ore
Nova Scotia	Halifax	756,000	21,425	1867	Iron and steel, fish, pulp and paper, coal, dairy products, cattle
Ontario	Toronto	6,961,000	412,582	1867	Autos, smelting and refining, iron and steel, cattle, dairy products, hydroelectric power, pulp and paper, nickel, uranium
Prince Edward Island	Charlottetown	109,000	2,184	1873	Fish, potatoes, dairy products, cattle
Quebec	Quebec	5,781,000	594,860	1867	Smelting and refining, pulp and paper, asbestos, dairy products, hogs, cattle, copper, hydroelectric power
Saskatchewan	Regina	955,000	251,700	1905	Oil, meat packing, wheat, cattle, uranium
Northwest Territories	Yellowknife	29,000	1,304,903	——	Gold, uranium, nickel, copper
Yukon Territory	Whitehorse	14,000	207,076	——	Silver, gold, lead, zinc

Credits

The sources for the illustrations in this book are shown below. Credits for pictures from left to right are separated by commas, top to bottom by dashes.

Cover—George Hunter
8, 9—Henry Groskinsky
11—Map by Bill Dove
15—Map by Rafael Palacios
16—Dan Weiner
17 through 21—Kryn Taconis
22, 23—Ted Russell
24—Margaret Bourke-White
25—National Film Board Photo by Kenneth Parks
26, 27—Courtesy Canadian Pacific
29—Map by Rafael D. Palacios
35—Public Archives of Canada
36—Courtesy Canadian Pacific
37—Ernest Brown Collection—Courtesy Canadian Pacific
38—Annan Photo Features, John Phillips—Brown Brothers
39—Alfred Eisenstaedt—Ralph Morse, Canada Wide-*Weekend Magazine*
40, 41—Bill Cadzow of Capital Press
46—Drawing by Ted Chambers
48, 49—Kryn Taconis
50—J. R. Eyerman
51—Ted Russell
52, 53—Kryn Taconis
54, 55—A. Y. Owen
56, 57—Richard Meek
58, 59—Kryn Taconis
65—Ted Russell
66 through 68—Kryn Taconis
69—Province of Quebec Film Bureau—National Film Board of Canada
70—Graphic Artists, Toronto
71—Kryn Taconis
72—George Silk
73—Richard Meek for SPORTS ILLUSTRATED
74—Alfred Eisenstaedt
81 through 83—Kryn Taconis
84, 85—Richard Meek for SPORTS ILLUSTRATED
86—Kryn Taconis
94, 95—Canada Wide-*Weekend Magazine*
96, 97—Kryn Taconis, Cornell Capa from Magnum—Kryn Taconis—Geoffrey James
102, 103—Richard Harrington
107—Map by Bill Dove
110—Carl Iwasaki
111—George Hunter
112, 113—Carl Mydans
114—Fritz Goro
115—Kryn Taconis
116—George Harris from Black Star
123—Robert W. Kelley
124—George Hunter
125—Ted Russell
126, 127—Robert W. Kelley
128, 129—Ted Russell
130—Robert C. Ragsdale
134—Royal Ontario Museum, University of Toronto
135—National Museum of Canada, Bulletin 119
137—Kryn Taconis
138—Robert C. Ragsdale
139—Kryn Taconis, Sam Tata—Sam Tata, Paul Gelinas
140—Tess Bourdreau—Ivor Sharp, Tess Bourdreau
141—Reproduced courtesy of National Gallery of Canada
142—Anthony Hayman courtesy the permanent collection of Hart House—Reproduced courtesy of National Gallery of Canada
143—Reproduced courtesy of National Gallery of Canada
144—Kryn Taconis
149—National Film Board of Canada
150, 151—J. R. Eyerman

ACKNOWLEDGMENTS

The editors of this book are indebted to Dennis Wrong, Professor of Sociology, New York University and to Stephen Clarkson, Associate Professor of Political Science, University of Toronto, who read and commented on the entire text; and to Alan Jarvis, Editor of *Canadian Art,* who gave valuable advice on portions of Chapter 9 and the Appendix.

Index

** This symbol in front of a page number indicates a photograph or painting of the subject mentioned.*

Production staff for Time Incorporated
John L. Hallenbeck (Vice President and Director of Production)
Robert E. Foy and Caroline Ferri
Text photocomposed under the direction of
Albert J. Dunn and Arthur J. Dunn

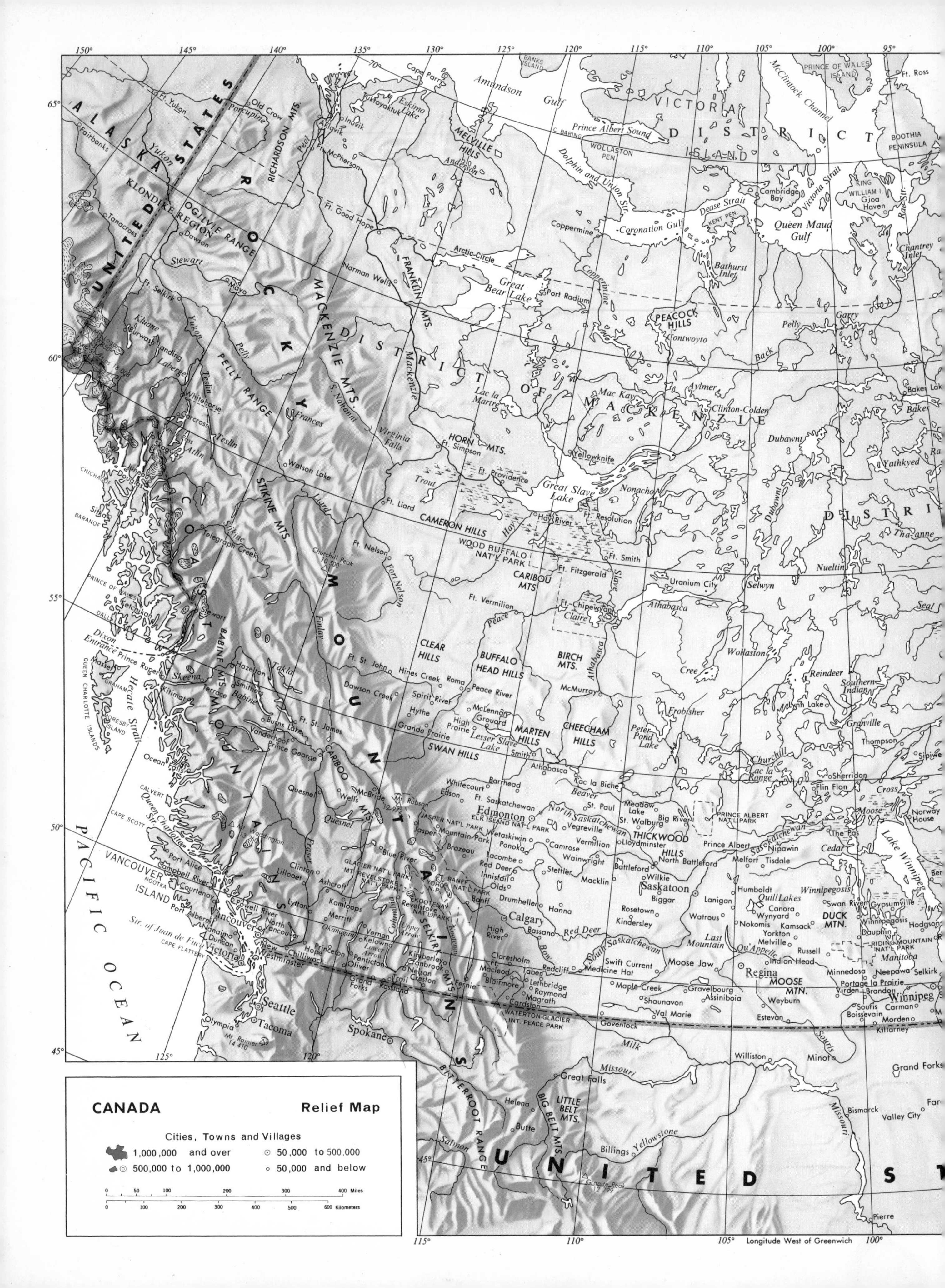
CANADA
Relief Map
Cities, Towns and Villages
1,000,000 and over
500,000 to 1,000,000
50,000 to 500,000
50,000 and below
0 50 100 200 300 400 Miles
0 100 200 300 400 500 600 Kilometers
Longitude West of Greenwich
ALASKA
UNITED STATES
DISTRICT OF MACKENZIE
VICTORIA ISLAND
DISTRICT
ROCKY MOUNTAINS
COAST MOUNTAINS
PACIFIC OCEAN
UNITED ST
Amundson Gulf
Prince Albert Sound
Dolphin and Union Str.
Coronation Gulf
Queen Maud Gulf
McClintock Channel
Victoria Strait
Dease Strait
Great Bear Lake
Great Slave Lake
Athabasca
Lake Winnipeg
RICHARDSON MTS.
OGILVIE RANGE
KLONDIKE REGION
PELLY RANGE
MACKENZIE MTS.
FRANKLIN MTS.
MELVILLE HILLS
HORN MTS.
CAMERON HILLS
STIKINE MTS.
CARIBOU MTS.
CLEAR HILLS
BUFFALO HEAD HILLS
BIRCH MTS.
MARTEN HILLS
CHEECHAM HILLS
SWAN HILLS
THICKWOOD HILLS
CARIBOO MTS.
SELKIRK MTS.
BITTERROOT RANGE
LITTLE BELT MTS.
BIG BELT MTS.
DUCK MTN.
MOOSE MTN.
PEACOCK HILLS
WOOD BUFFALO NAT'L PARK
JASPER NAT'L PARK
PRINCE ALBERT NAT'L PARK
WATERTON GLACIER INT. PEACE PARK
RIDING MOUNTAIN NAT'L PARK
VANCOUVER ISLAND
QUEEN CHARLOTTE ISLANDS
Hecate Strait
Dixon Entrance
Str. of Juan de Fuca
Fairbanks
Old Crow
Dawson
Whitehorse
Inuvik
Aklavik
Tuktoyaktuk
Ft. McPherson
Ft. Good Hope
Norman Wells
Coppermine
Port Radium
Yellowknife
Ft. Simpson
Ft. Providence
Hay River
Ft. Resolution
Ft. Smith
Ft. Liard
Ft. Nelson
Watson Lake
Uranium City
Ft. Chipewyan
Ft. St. John
Dawson Creek
Peace River
Grande Prairie
Prince Rupert
Prince George
Edmonton
Calgary
Vancouver
Victoria
Seattle
Tacoma
Spokane
Red Deer
Lethbridge
Medicine Hat
Saskatoon
Regina
Moose Jaw
Prince Albert
Winnipeg
Brandon
Flin Flon
Great Falls
Helena
Butte
Billings
Minot
Bismarck
Williston
Grand Forks
Pierre
Yellowstone
Missouri
Milk
Churchill
Saskatchewan
Yukon
Liard
Peace
Fraser
Mackenzie
Arctic Circle
Mt. Robson 12,972
Mt. Waddington 13,260
Mt. Rainier 14,410
Churchill Peak 10,500
Granite Peak 12,799